# EVACUEE

*a Child's Life and Love in Victoria*

by

# John Napier-Hemy

*1: VR1993.59.3 N309, RMS Queen Elizabeth, 1942*

This picture and that of the Weser on p.85 are used with thanks to the
Canadian Forces Base Esquimalt Naval & Military Museum

# Evacuee

by John Napier-Hemy

Copyright © John Napier-Hemy 2018

    Author:    John Napier-Hemy

    Publisher:  Rutherford Press

    For information, contact:

        Rutherford Press,
        PO Box 648
        Qualicum Beach, BC, Canada V9K 1A0
        info@rutherfordpress.ca

        https://rutherfordpress.ca

Printed in the United States of America and Canada.
All rights reserved. No part of this book may be reproduced in whole or in part, materially or digitally, including photocopying, without the express written permission of the author or publisher.
        ISBN (book)  # 978-1-988739-34-2

        ISBN (ebook) # 978-1-988739-35-9

## *Dedication*

I am dedicating this book to my late father, Hubert John Napier-Hemy. He was an Englishman who had taken to heart the maxim famously stated by Vice Admiral Horatio Nelson at outset of the Battle of Trafalgar in 1805. What he is believed to have said was, "England expects that every man this day will do his duty." My father lived his life in accordance with his belief in duty, and it is perhaps no coincidence that his first tour of duty during my lifetime took place in the city of Nelson, BC.

I was born in 1931, shortly after my parents moved from San Francisco to a large home on Head Street in Esquimalt. The Great Depression was in full swing, and my parents had no money to pay board to my grandparents who owned the house. The only work my father could find was as a garage mechanic in Nelson, B.C. I was too little to understand why he was not at home with us, but later learned that he was spending winter days in an unheated garage to make enough money to send home to my mother.

His first break from this grueling routine came in 1936 when he was able to obtain work at Thornycroft, a shipbuilding company located on the Thames River not far from the city of Reading in Berkshire, England.

We moved from Victoria to Reading. He had earlier been trained in England as a marine engineer, and at Thornycroft was able to put his education and training into practice designing motor torpedo boats. The British government foresaw at that time that war with Germany was inevitable, and that Britain would be able to blockade continental Europe with fast attack boats designed to keep German shipping out of the English Channel and the Atlantic.

War did break out in 1939, and by August of 1940 it appeared that Nazi Germany was winning the Battle of Britain, and his duty to family encouraged him to arrange for tickets for my mother, my sister and myself on the *Duchess of Athol,* leaving Liverpool and bound for Halifax in Nova Scotia. The *Duchess* and her sister ship *City of Benares* were the last two ships carrying child evacuees to safety in North America. The *Benares* was sunk by U-boats mid-Atlantic with practically all the child passengers drowned. The *Athol* made it, and my father had thus secured our safety in Canada, living in Halifax with my mother's sister and her family,

My father's decision to remain alone in our house in Reading must have come close to ending his life. The Luftwaffe bombed Thornycroft on several occasions, a tempting target for German bombs partly owing to its convenient proximity to the factory where the British were building Spitfire fighter planes.

*2: Elizabeth in the garden enjoying the late summer sun*

# Contents

First Form .................................................................................. 1
Blackout .................................................................................. 15
Beliefs .................................................................................. 25
On Being Hip .................................................................................. 41
Return to Victoria .................................................................................. 52
Glenlyon .................................................................................. 58
The Admirals House .................................................................................. 74
Christmas in Victoria .................................................................................. 86
Lessons on the Farm .................................................................................. 98
The World is Coming Apart .................................................................................. 110
Being in the Movies .................................................................................. 124
Oak Bay .................................................................................. 138
Building Airplanes .................................................................................. 164
Aunt Madge's History of Victoria .................................................................................. 179
The Wonderful Land of Moo .................................................................................. 204
A Summer of Action .................................................................................. 223
Being a Hero on Mount Douglas .................................................................................. 231
The Problem With Long Pants .................................................................................. 244
Shocking Bad Taste .................................................................................. 253
Is the War Over Already? .................................................................................. 266
*Figures* .................................................................................. 283

# CHAPTER 1

# FIRST FORM

*"Sunday, September 3,1939. Everyone who is old enough who was there remembers exactly what they were doing at that moment."*

:John Boorman at the introduction of his film *"Hope and Glory"*.

> "I am speaking to you from the Cabinet Room at 10 Downing Street. This morning the British Ambassador in Berlin handed the German Government an official note stating that unless we heard from them by eleven o'clock, they were prepared to withdraw their troops from Poland, a state of war would exist between us. I have to tell you now that no such undertaking has been received, and consequently this country is at war with Germany."

: Prime Minister Neville Chamberlain, 3 September 1939

"Bloody Huns!" my father said. The lines in his face were drawn and tight. He had fought in the First World War. He had been a naval officer and had fought the Germans in the Battle of Jutland. The Germans had been defeated, but now they would have to be defeated all over again. "Have they learned nothing?"

"Weakling!" My mother flung a contemptuous glance at the radio. That was what she thought of Prime Minister Chamberlain, the man who had just been speaking. A weak little man who had carried his umbrella to Munich and let Hitler bully him. He had let Hitler take Czechoslovakia and now Hitler thought he could get away with anything.

I heard the word *war* and I knew what was about to happen. The Germans would bomb us to bits just as they had done to Poland. Our home would be blown up, my parents would be blown up, my beloved garden would be blown up and I would be blown up and that would be that. I waited. My two-year old sister, Elizabeth, did not know that she was about to be blown up. She was not even listening to the radio. She was in the garden enjoying the late summer sun. She was sniffing flowers and running after a butterfly. I envied her and wished I could be that carefree.

I looked around me. Our living room at Sunny Corner was filled with beautiful old furniture. There were seascapes on the walls and an enormous grandfather clock. There were French doors with leaded glass windows leading into a large garden. On one side of the lawn there were flower beds filled with lupines, columbines, and delphiniums. Most of them had gone to seed now, but they had been glorious earlier in the summer. Of course all of this would be blown up along with the house.

Then an air raid siren sounded. I had never heard one before but I knew immediately what it was and what it meant. The German bombers were right overhead getting ready to unload their bombs. My parents brought Elizabeth inside and then we went through a trap-door in the floor of the kitchen and down a few steps into a dark, dank crawl space.

It smelled horrible down there so it must have been right next to our cesspool. I knew what was going to happen down there when the Germans dropped their bombs We would be crushed underneath our own house. Or worse still – drowned in our own cesspool.

Then the air raid siren sounded again. But this time it sounded different. It sounded reassuring as though nothing was going to happen after all.

"That's the All Clear," my father explained.

"What does that mean?"

"It means it was just a practice. They want us to know what the air raid siren sounds like and what we are supposed to do when we hear it."

Just a practice? Did that mean that we weren't going to be blown up right away? Did it mean that the next time we heard the siren we would really be blown up?

At bedtime I put on my pajamas and came downstairs to the kitchen. My mother had made me a nice hot glass of Ovaltine. Before I went to bed my mother and father both told me not to forget my prayers. That was reassuring because sometimes they argued about which were the best prayers. You see, my mother was an Anglican and my father was a Catholic and they had different prayers. But they both agreed on a prayer called, "Now I lay me".

Before I got into bed I kneeled at the side of my bed facing my pillow and prayed:

> *Now I lay me down to sleep*
>
> *I pray the Lord my soul to keep.*
>
> *If I should die before I wake*
>
> *I pray the Lord my soul to take.*

The prayer was reassuring and the Ovaltine had made me sleepy. In no time at all I was fast asleep. It had been an exhausting day. When I woke up in the morning I was still there. I hadn't been blown up and God hadn't taken my soul anywhere.

When I got up I stopped thinking about it quite so much. There were other things requiring my attention. One of them was school. I was about to begin school – a real school! I had gone to school the year before but it wasn't a real school. It was a kindergarten run by nuns. I had learned to read there

## First Form

but they didn't have enough books and I had wound up making a nuisance of myself. I had embarrassed myself because Mother Superior had to teach me to wipe my bum with the shiny, slippery paper they had in the outdoor toilet. I had fallen in love with a beautiful blonde girl named Joyce who refused to notice me. To gain her attention I had catapulted myself out of a swing and knocked myself unconscious on the playground. When I regained consciousness I had expected to see Joyce standing over me with a sweet smile, but instead there was a nun hovering over me like a huge bat and she wasn't smiling.

I hadn't liked going to the convent kindergarten. The outdoor bathroom was always cold. The toilet frightened me because the tank was high up on the ceiling and I had to pull on the chain several times to make it work. I was afraid the tank might come loose from the wall and fall on top of my head. And the dogs on the way to school had frightened me. There were several big dogs in one block and they barked at me every morning. And the nuns frightened me. I was afraid that one of them might lose her hat in the wind and I would have had to look at her bald head.

But now my year in Kindergarten was over and I was ready for a real school. My parents had enrolled me in the first form of Reading Grammar School. School. When I got up the morning after the war broke out I put on my new school clothes - grey short pants, a grey jacket, an itchy grey flannel shirt, a striped blue and white school tie, a school cap with a

## First Form

badge on front that said "RGS" and shiny black shoes. I walked to my new school all by myself and was delighted to find that all the other boys were dressed in exactly the same way as I was.

My First Form teacher was a lady named Miss Riley. I liked her because she wasn't a nun and wasn't afraid to smile. On the first day of school we had to tell her where we lived, and then she told us which *House* we were in. I was in *County House* because our home was outside the Reading city limits. That meant that my parents had to buy me a football jersey with horizontal purple and white stripes. I felt proud when I wore it and I felt that the other boys in County House were my friends. It was all so exciting that I almost forgot about the war.

On the second day of school Miss Riley took us to an assembly. We marched single file into a huge hall, and, because we were the smallest boys in the school, we had to stand at the very front. We stood in silence when the headmaster walked in. His name was Mr. Peach. I thought that was a nice name for a headmaster but he looked very stern and strict.

Mr. Peach had a lot to say about the war. "The Nazis...or should I say the Nasties?" He paused to give us time to laugh at his joke. "The Nazis have rained destruction on the innocent people of Poland and now they want to do the

First Form

same to us. But this time they will find that they have bitten off a little more than they can chew. Hnnh!"

Mr. Peach made a little nasal sound at the end of each important sentence. "Hnnh" meant that we were supposed to agree with what he said.

Then he told us about the glorious British Empire and how Great Britain stood for everything that was good and right. He ended by talking about how air raid drills were to be conducted and about gas masks. He even had a gas mask in his hand to show us what he was talking about. And then to my alarm he put on the gas mask to show us how to wear one. All of a sudden he was transformed from a man into a monster with two dead-looking eyes and a huge snout. It was a frightening sight and I was glad when he took it off again. At the end of his speech Mr. Peach led us in three cheers for Great Britain and the British Empire.

"Hip hip hooray!"

"Hip hip hooray!"

"Hip hip hooray!"

When the assembly was over Miss Riley led us back to our classroom. We were filled with ourselves. If any German soldiers had showed up that day we would have shown them what it meant to be British.

First Form

The following day we were issued with our own gas masks. Miss Riley marched us outside to a building with a round corrugated metal roof. Then we had to march down some steps and sit on two benches facing each other. We sat and waited until Mr. Peach arrived with instructions.

"Pay attention, boys. Put the gas masks over your head. Clip them on at the back and breathe in gently. Don't be frightened. You'll get used to it, and it may save your life some day; hnnh!"

I was terrified. I was convinced that I would suffocate as soon as I put on the mask. But I did as I was told and learned to breathe in and breathe out. The big thing was not to panic and not be frightened at the sight of the other boys who suddenly looked like Martians.

The gas masks got hot and clammy after only a few minutes, and it was a huge relief when we were allowed to take them off. When we did we smiled at each other. We had completed our initiation and would know what to do the next time.

I got used to wearing a gas mask and I got used to the air raid drills. I kept waiting for the Germans to bomb us but they didn't. I stopped thinking about being blown to bits and learned how to be a pupil in the First Form of Reading Grammar School.

First Form

One thing I learned was that the playground was just as important as the classroom. The playground was where I was expected to learn Character. Fighting was encouraged but it always had to be a fair fight. There were unwritten rules. You could wrestle with your opponent or you could have a fist fight, but the rule was that you could only fight with someone approximately your own size. If you started a fight you had to make sure that you weren't a lot bigger than your opponent or you would be considered a bully. If you wanted to have a fist fight the rule was that you could strike your opponent on the body, but not on the face. Striking your opponent below the belt was forbidden and considered shameful into the bargain.

"Do you want to fight, Titch?"

The other boys called me *Titch* because I was so small. The smallest boy in the whole school in fact. That meant that every time I fought it was with someone slightly larger than myself.

"You're a good sport, Titch."

That was my reward for being small. I was automatically considered a good sport, and, because I was strong and wiry, I frequently won.

"The British always fight fair," Miss Riley told us. What she was telling us was that Germany, which had quickly overcome Poland in a one-sided war, did not fight fair. They were bullies but we could take pride in fighting by the rules.

That was how I learned to be British. I had to fight fair, be a good sport and not bully smaller children. There was one more thing I had to learn and that was to stand up to authority. Not too often but just enough to show that I wasn't a mindless automaton like Hitler's Nazi followers.

With that in mind I carefully bit off the end of an eraser, waited until Miss Riley was looking in my direction, and then flung it across the room at one of the other boys. I missed but the point was to catch Miss Riley's attention. I succeeded.

"It's not permissible to send eraser pieces flying across the classroom, Hemy. With a well-placed shot you could puncture another boy's eardrum. You have made the janitor's job that much harder and of course you have wasted rubber. It's very difficult to obtain rubber from the colonies these days with the Germans sinking ships all over the globe. There are other reasons, I'm sure, that Mr. Peach will be only too pleased to explain to you. Please excuse yourself and report to him with this note."

I took the note that Miss Riley had scribbled for me and headed out the classroom door and onto the parade square. I had achieved what I had set out to do but now I was terrified. Mr. Peach's office was situated at the other end of the parade square. I knocked. Mr. Peach came to the door.

"What's your name, boy?"

"Hemy, sir."

"Well, don't just stand there wasting my time. What do you want?"

I handed Mr. Peach the note that Miss Riley had written. As Mr. Peach read the note I had the opportunity to observe him at first hand. He was tall, angular and athletic-looking. His hair was Brylcreemed into place. Just like my father and just like King George VI. He wore a checkered jacket with large leather patches on the elbow and a slightly motheaten pullover underneath his jacket. A quick glance around his study revealed a tennis racket, a cricket bat, and leather-bound copies of Shakespeare, Sir Walter Scott and G.A. Henty - tales of character and courage. When he had read and re-read Miss Riley's note he clenched his jaw so hard that the veins in his neck stood out. His face reddened.

"What did you say your name was?"

"Hemy, sir."

"Then presumably your father must be Mr. Hemy."

"Yes, sir."

"Do you think your father would be happy to know that you are paying me a visit this morning?"

"Yes, sir. I mean no, sir."

"Are you aware that Miss Riley is the most kindly and understanding teacher you could possibly have to instruct you? She is absolutely wonderful. And yet you have failed to appreciate your good fortune - hnnh! Instead you have had the temerity to impose on her good will by behaving like a young hooligan while she is attempting to impart her scholarship into your empty head - hnnh!"

Mr. Peach's face kept getting redder and a small fleck of white spittle had appeared at the corner of his mouth. He walked over to the corner of his study and selected the shortest of several canes.

"Place both hands on the back of this chair, Hemy."

By now I was in an agony of anticipation. Mr. Peach came up behind me and carefully folded back the hem of my jacket so that he would be able to enjoy a clear swing at my bottom. First he gently tapped my backside with the end of the cane

"Are you sure you don't have anything next to your underwear, Hemy?"

"Yes sir. I'm sure I don't."

"One of the older boys came to see me last week. He had sought to soften the blow by placing an exercise book in between his underwear and his pants. A despicable ruse - hnnh? I have to tell you that he has only just been released from hospital after a rather lengthy stay. Now you're sure there's nothing there, Hemy?"

"No sir. I mean yes sir."

I looked up at a clock on the wall. A good five minutes had elapsed since I was admitted to Mr. Peach's study. By now I was sweating. Perhaps he intended to let me go with a lecture. Finally after a pause that felt like a million years Mr. Peach's cane connected with my bottom. Crack! I had not even imagined that the pain would be so intense. He swung again. Crack!

"Now go back to Miss Riley's room. You can return her note with my initials so that she will know you've been disciplined appropriately. And please don't come back here wasting my time again – hnnh!"

"No sir."

I bit my lower lip and choked back the tears. Then I swaggered back to my classroom. The hem of my jacket was still upturned. I was entitled to leave it that way until the end of the day. It was my badge of courage, a sign that I had been caned and not shed a tear. The other boys nodded their approval. I had earned their respect. I had learned to conduct myself in the way that a British schoolboy should – accepting the fairness of the punishment and taking it cheerfully.

After that encounter I worked very hard in class. I wanted to impress Miss Riley with my good intentions. When I received my first report card I was thrilled to see that I had come first in my form in Geography with 87%. Miss Riley had written that I was "an apt and enthusiastic young scholar". My love of Geography never left me.

## CHAPTER 2

## BLACKOUT

My father covered all the windows at Sunny Corner with heavy black paper. He had to do this very quickly or else the German bombers flying overhead would see the light at night and drop bombs on us. It had to be perfect. If he let just a little light show through people would think he belonged to the Nazi Fifth Column and was deliberately leading the German bombers to Reading. The Fifth Column was supposedly composed of Englishmen who agreed with what the Germans were doing and wanted to help them. They were traitors.

Just to make sure that people obeyed the rules about light there was an ARP man right at the foot of our road. ARP stood for Air Raid Precautions. The ARP man was a gentleman who was too old to serve in the armed forces but wanted to help the War Effort. He wore a helmet, carried a gas mask and stood beside a barrel of sand with a shovel stuck in it. If there were any small fires left over from a bombing, he could shovel sand onto them to put them out. When he wasn't standing there he walked around to the houses at night to make sure they were properly blacked out.

*3: First he dug a hole in the spinney*

As soon as my father had finished putting the black paper in place he had to build an air raid shelter. First he dug a hole in the spinney as far away from the house as possible. Then he got some sandbags from the ARP and built up the walls of the shelter. The sand bags would protect us from any pieces of bombs that might go flying after they exploded. Then he completed the roof by installing curved sheets of corrugated metal. That was to keep us dry at night and protect us from any bomb pieces that might fall right on top of us. Then he built a couple of wooden benches so we would have somewhere to sit during an air raid.

The air raid siren sounded just about every night. We had to get out of bed, put on dressing gowns and march through our garden to the spinney and sit in the shelter until we heard the "all clear". Then we would trudge back into the house. Once inside my mother made Ovaltine so we would feel sleepy before we went back to bed. It was always the same. We listened for bombs but we never heard any. I decided the ARP must be sounding the siren just so we'd have the practice of going in and out of our shelters.

The worst part of the air raid drills was having to get out of a warm, cozy bed after I'd already gone to sleep. Then when we got to the shelter we had to share it with slugs. This was because our shelter was in the spinney where my father made compost with the garden cuttings and lawn clippings. The slugs loved it there.

"Hubert, there are slugs out here!" My mother was revolted by the sight of slugs.

"Well, there's nothing I can do about that. It's damp and they enjoy eating the vegetation. Look at it this way. They're eating all those stinging nettles you hate so much."

My mother wasn't impressed by my father's cheeriness or his argument. She loathed the sight of slugs and that was that.

My father had an important job. He was a marine engineer and he worked at a shipyard called Thorneycroft's on the River Thames. Thorneycroft's made motor torpedo boats or MTBs as they were called for short.

*4 A proud father*

My father was proud of his work.

"If Jerry tries to get his ships out of his harbours the MTBs will come along and sink them with torpedoes. The MTBs can race across the Channel and back to home port in no time at all. They're very fast."

I admired my father and the work he was doing. If anyone could stop the German Navy he could.

Blackout

My father must have been making a good salary because when my birthday came along he bought me a train set. It was a wonderful set with several feet of track, a trestle, a tunnel, trees and a railroad station. There was a shiny red engine, cars to carry coal and chemicals and several passenger cars. The passenger cars carried the names of the British railroads. There was Midland, Great Northern and Great Western. My mind filled with fantasies of destinations, stations, tunnels and great billows of smoke coming from powerful steam engines.

One day there was a knock on the door. My mother answered it. There was an important-looking gentleman accompanied by two boys dressed in grey jackets and short pants, just as I was.

"This is John and Michael Delaney, ma'm. They will be billeted with you. Run back to the car and pick up your suitcases, boys." Moments later the Delaney brothers reappeared with their belongings and the gentleman who had brought them to our home disappeared. There were no pleases, no thank yous, just the announcement that the Delaney brothers would be living with us.

My mother shrugged her shoulders and led them to my bedroom. They were to share my bed and I was to sleep in a canvas cot. That evening at dinner my father explained the situation. John and Michael had been evacuated from London. The government was afraid that the Germans were about to bomb the huge shipyards in London and they were evacuating the children from London to towns where they would be safe.

"Of course this will be difficult for us but it's even more difficult for John and Michael. They will be away from their home and family."

My mother did not look impressed. The Delaney boys pouted. Elizabeth looked wide-eyed as though she didn't know what to expect. Dinner was a strain. The Delaneys hardly knew how to hold a knife and fork and when they ate it was with loud, smacking noises. They had runny noses that they wiped with their sleeves. My mother winced.

"And what are your favourite school subjects?" My father was trying to make conversation.

" 'ate school!"

I had to listen carefully to what the Delaneys were saying as they dropped all their 'h's when they spoke. Fortunately they weren't all that interested in conversation.

What did interest them was my train set. Their eyes lit up as soon as they saw it.

"Coo! A train!"

The Delaneys did not ask me if they could play with my train. They simply assumed that it was there for their amusement. I had been using the switches on the track to

*5: The Delaney boys taking over*

guide the engine safely into the station. The Delaneys used the switches to throw the engine off the tracks. When they tired of this activity they set up the cars on the track so the engine would run into them at full speed.

"'ere. Not that car. This one. Now 'it it with the engine, stupid."

John Delaney gave the orders and Michael had to obey. If Michael didn't obey John punched him.

"There's to be no hitting," my father told them. "That's a rule."

John Delaney obeyed my father until bedtime. Then after lights out he felt free to bully Michael as much as he wanted.

Sometimes he twisted Michael's arm and pinned him down on the bed. Sometimes he shoved a pillow over his head. Not long enough to suffocate him but just long enough to frighten him. What was worse was that John liked to stick his finger in his bum to make it smelly and then shove it into Michael's nose. It was disgusting. I didn't complain to John about it. He was quite a bit bigger than I was and I didn't want him doing the same horrible thing to me.

On Sunday Mrs. Delaney came to visit the boys. They sat in the living room with her while my mother made tea.

"Do you care for a cup of tea, Mrs. Delaney?"

"Awright, Love. 'ow are my boys?"

"They seem to be adjusting to the change quite well," my mother lied.

"John's a bully. If 'e starts throwin' 'is weight around, just smack him one. Know what I mean?"

My mother nodded.

"Don't be gettin' soft on Michael, neither. 'e looks like a choir boy, but 'e's a sneaky little bugger."

My mother did not like Mrs. Delaney. She didn't appreciate Mrs. Delaney's rough language, and winced at the sight of her coarse facial hairs. And she hated having to be polite to her. She was so obviously common.

Worse still the Delaneys were Catholic. This meant frequent visits from the priest, an anaemic-looking man in black clerical garb who sat in the living room and warned the Delaney brothers about the dangers of sin. The priest looked bored with his job and the Delaney boys looked bored as they listened to him. My mother did not offer the priest tea.

The Delaney boys played on the street on the weekend. They either kicked a soccer ball or used the opportunity to bully an Italian boy who had been billeted with one of our neighbours. They called the Italian boy "Sausages" because his mother brought him a special treat of Italian sausage every Sunday.

"'ey, Sausages. 'oo says you should even be allowed 'ere? Why ain't you interned with all them other wops? You're an enemy alien is what you are. Go back where you belong with Mussolini and all them other fat wops. 'itler lover!"

As soon as they had poor Sausages reduced to tears they went back to their soccer practice.

One day a man from the Government came and told the Delaney boys to pack. They weren't safe here in Reading because the Germans might decide to bomb the shipyards. They were to be sent out into the countryside instead.

They left as quickly as they had arrived. I could hardly believe my good fortune. But then I looked at my train. The tracks were twisted, the clockwork motor on the engine was broken and the passenger cars were dented from the many collisions with the engine. It would never be the same. I would have been quite happy if the Germans had dropped one of their bombs on the Delaneys as soon as they left the house.

## CHAPTER 3

# BELIEFS

I liked Reading Grammar School a whole lot better than the convent school except for one thing. At the convent school all the other children were Catholic so it wasn't something I had to think about. At my new school none of the other boys were Catholic. Just me. So I thought about that a lot.

I thought about it the most when we had to stand for the Lord's Prayer in the morning. My father had told me that I was not to say the last sentence of the prayer because that was something the Anglicans had added on at the time of Queen Elizabeth. What they had added at the end went: "For thine is the kingdom, the power and the glory / Forever and ever / Amen."

"It was really Queen Elizabeth who wanted people to pray about her power and glory," my father explained.

I didn't reply because I didn't understand, but every morning when we stood for the Lord's Prayer I stopped right after I had said, "But deliver us from evil". I have to admit that I mouthed the words because I didn't want to be conspicuous, but I didn't actually say them. When I

Beliefs

gradually started to think about the words I had to agree with my father. Power and glory didn't seem to be the right things to put into a prayer. I wound up feeling a little superior to all the Anglicans around me, but I also felt very much alone.

My mother was an Anglican and my father was a Catholic. Elizabeth was too little to be anything, so there was really just my father and I who were Catholics.

"Catholics can expect to be persecuted," my father said. "King Henry VIII beheaded them and Queen Elizabeth burned them at the stake. But we should take joy in our persecution. If we bear our persecution bravely there will be a special place for us in Heaven."

I listened but I didn't like what I was hearing. I didn't really want to be persecuted no matter how good it might be for me after I was dead. It just didn't seem fair.

One good thing about the war was that Guy Fawkes Day was cancelled. Guy Fawkes Day was held every November 5. The way it worked was that someone built a huge bonfire on a field close to our home. Then in the evening the Fire Department came along and set the tower alight. Then the children threw their "Guys" onto the bonfire. The "Guys" were effigies of Guy Fawkes, a traitor who had tried to blow up the Parliament Buildings in London. They were made of old clothes stuffed with newspapers and rags. As the Guys burned the children chanted a verse.

Beliefs

> Please to remember the fifth of November,
>
> Gunpowder, treason, and plot.
>
> I see no reason why gunpowder treason
>
> Should ever be forgot.

My father didn't like Guy Fawkes Day. "Catholics were persecuted in England and Guy Fawkes was trying to help them. The gunpowder never went off, but they tried Guy Fawkes and executed him anyway. Hung, drawn and quartered!"

My father shuddered as he described Guy Fawkes' fate. I didn't know what "hung, drawn and quartered" meant but I was pretty sure it was awful. So that was why I was glad when Guy Fawkes Day was cancelled. I wanted to see a bonfire but I didn't want to think of poor Guy Fawkes being persecuted and then executed in such a terrible way. The real reason it was cancelled, of course, was because a bonfire would have shown the German bombers exactly where Reading was.

I was excited when Christmas rolled around. I was pretty sure I would get a few things to add to my train set – tunnels, bridges, trees and cows and stuff like that. And I did. But I got something else as well. It was a book called "The Martyrdom of Poland". I didn't know what "martyrdom" meant but I soon found out. The book was filled with pictures of the German invasion of Poland. Real photographs. It showed terrible things. There were photographs of buildings burning in Warsaw. There were photographs of German soldiers attacking people in the streets, and photographs of people being lined up and shot by the Gestapo. Some of them were Catholic priests. At the very end there were photographs of Polish airmen who had escaped to Britain and were now flying Spitfires for the Royal Air Force. Brave and gallant men!

This book didn't seem to me like a proper kind of Christmas present. I had thought that Christmas presents were supposed to make me feel happy. But this present made me feel sad and afraid. I was afraid that if the Germans invaded the Gestapo would hunt me down because I was Catholic. I put the book away in my bookshelf and never opened it again. I started to have nightmares about the Gestapo. I dreamed about them searching our house and finding me.

"So zere you are, you little sneak. Ve haff special plans for Catholics. Ja!"

Then I would wake up and I would be safe in my bed. But the Gestapo would be back again the following night.

I tried to avoid having serious conversations with my father. He was fine if he was telling jokes, but I never knew when he was going to say something gloomy about Catholics being persecuted.

Beliefs

All through the winter we went out to our shelter every time we heard the air raid siren. But we never heard any bombs and we never saw any bombers overhead. It didn't seem as though there was really a war at all. The man who read the news on the BBC called this quiet period "The Phoney War".

When spring came we took a picnic lunch to Sonning Village just outside Reading. Sonning was a village built right beside the River Thames. There were whitewashed buildings with tall gables and dark wooden boards dividing up the buildings into sections. Vines covered the walls. Everything about Sonning Village seemed old.

"Sonning Village was built in Tudor times," my father told me, but I wasn't listening. I ran first to the side of the river to watch the graceful swans teaching the baby cygnets to scoop up weeds from the water. Then I ran to Sonning Bridge where there was a footpath directly above a waterfall. I thought that Sonning Village was the most beautiful place I had ever seen in my life.

What interested me most were the locks. If a boat was headed upstream the captain would steer it into a chamber in the river called a lock. Then a gate would close behind the boat and the lock would fill with water from the water upstream. Then the boat would rise to the same level as the higher part of the river and another gate would open to allow the boat to proceed on its journey. The sound and sight of the rushing water excited my imagination.

The gates were controlled by the lock-keeper, an elderly man with a grizzled white beard. My father went and spoke to him, and the next thing I knew I was turning the wheel that opened and closed the gates all by myself. I opened the upper gate and the next thing I knew the boat below me was swirling in a rush of water and foam. The waterfall stopped just as suddenly as it had started and the boat continued on its journey up the Thames. I felt powerful to have made all this happen, but I was only allowed one turn.

"Time to sit down for lunch," my mother announced. We sat down beside the river while my mother laid out our picnic on a tablecloth she had brought with her for the occasion.

It all seemed so magical and I was ready to believe that there was no war at all. If that was what I thought I was sadly mistaken. On May 10 the Germans invaded Holland, Belgium and France. Their sudden offensive was called a Blitzkrieg which meant "Lightning War". Their forces advanced so fast that an effective defense was impossible. It was an emergency. Winston Churchill immediately replaced Neville Chamberlain as Prime Minister. Churchill smoked a cigar and looked as though he really meant business.

To my surprise my father cheered up almost immediately. He had been so gloomy during the early part of the war and now he seemed filled with energy.

## Beliefs

"Chin up," my father said. "Never mind the war. We're going on another picnic."

I didn't understand the change but I think it must have been something to do with Churchill. If Churchill could stand up to the Germans then so could we.

My farther took us up the Thames in the opposite direction from Sonning Village for our next picnic. It was a warm, sunny day and my father had chosen a beautiful picnic site beneath a weeping willow tree. My parents had invited my best friend, Freddy Price, to come with us, and my father had arranged a special treat. He had rented a little boat called a punt.

First my father and I went out in the punt and he showed me how to steer it. The punt came with a long pole that he pushed into the water until it hit the river bottom. With every push the punt went further into the river. It looked so easy. Then it was my turn. Freddy Price and I got into the punt and I seized the pole. I pushed it into the river bottom and the punt went sailing ahead. This was so easy and so much fun. But when I tried to pull the pole out of the water for the next push something went wrong. The pole was stuck. I hung onto the pole while the punt kept going farther out into the river. The next thing I knew I was in the water flailing away in the direction of the shore. I didn't know how to swim, but I was close enough to the shore to grab some tree roots and pull myself out of the water.

Beliefs

Freddy Price was still in the punt and heading slowly downstream without a pole. My father had to act fast. He pulled off his shoes and pants and headed into the river. A few strokes and he was able to grab the end of the punt and bring Freddy into shore. I was soaking wet, my father was soaking wet and Freddy was shivering with fear. After my father had dried himself off and Freddy had stopped shaking we all had a good laugh while my mother was hauling the sandwiches out of the picnic basket. It was a wonderful picnic, but I felt a little ashamed that I hadn't handled the punt properly.

In June the Germans had moved so quickly through the north of France that the British Army was being pushed right up against the English Channel. They were in danger of being wiped out. Miraculously hundreds of boats assembled at a place called Dunkirk on the French coast and rescued most of the British troops.

But now we were in real danger. The Germans controlled the north of France they could launch an attack on Britain at any time.

Churchill got on the radio to address the nation. We sat in the living room and listened just as we had listened to Chamberlain at the beginning of the war.

"We shall fight on the beaches, we shall fight on the landing grounds, we shall fight in the fields and in the streets, we shall fight in the hills, we shall never surrender…."

Beliefs

It was electrifying. This wonderful man, Churchill, was now our leader in the fight against Germany. In my mind I was already standing on the beach ready to give my life for my country.

The next morning Mr. Peach called us all to an assembly.

"We will all be tested, hnnh! We must never flinch in our struggle against Germany. We must show them what Englishmen are made of, hnnh! Englishmen never flee from the enemy and never surrender. We can do no better than to follow the example of our Prime Minister, the Right Honourable Winston Churchill."

We all sang "There'll Always Be An England." After Three Cheers for England the assembly ended with "God Save the King".

Our chests filled with pride. At recess we hatched great plans for defending our country. We had no weapons, but we could run to farmyards and grab pitchforks for jabbing at the Germans. And if we died we would have died bravely.

When school ended for the summer my father had a plan for our vacation. We were to take the train to St. Ives in Cornwall.

"How's your Arithmetic, John? See if you can figure this one out. Are you ready?"

I groaned inwardly. Arithmetic was my worst subject.

Beliefs

"Ready."

My father began and I listened intently, trying to concentrate.

> As I was going to St. Ives
>
> I met a man with seven wives,
>
> Each wife had seven cats
>
> And each cat had seven kits
>
> Kits, cats, man and wives,
>
> How many going to St. Ives?

I grabbed a pencil and paper and started work. I didn't know my seven times tables so the task seemed almost impossible. But I had to solve it. What if I failed and my father decided not to take us to St. Ives after all?

"Give up?"

"I'm afraid so. It just seems like too many kits."

"The answer is one."

I looked at my father in amazement. How could that be?

"You see," my father said, "only I was going to Saint Ives. All the others were coming from St. Ives."

He had tricked me. I was annoyed with myself for being fooled. But then all I could think about was our trip to St.

Beliefs

Ives. The vacation was magical. We stayed with my Great Aunt Winnie. She lived at 7 Belair Terrace in a house that was so tiny that you could almost touch both walls of the living room if you stretched your arms out as far as you could. There were three storeys, and if you went to the very top there was a studio where Aunt Winnie kept all her paints and canvasses. She was an artist. There was a huge window in her studio where you could look out onto the blue waters of Carbis Bay. All along the beach were palm trees. The sun was shining and it was warm. I could hardly believe it. We had been transported into a wonderful tropical world. All I could think about was getting to the beach..

The next day I ran down to Porthmeor Beach with a bucket and a net. There were shrimp in the tidal pools and I was determined to catch enough for a meal.

"Please keep an eye on Elizabeth. I don't want her falling into the water."

My mother and Elizabeth had followed me to the beach. My mother sat on a rock. She was wearing a dress that she called a "summer frock" and Elizabeth, who was still only two, was tottering unevenly toward me.

"Always a fly in the ointment," I grumbled to myself.

But I was able to keep an eye on Elizabeth and net shrimp at the same time. My reward came at supper time. My mother boiled my shrimps for me. They had turned from a ghostly

Beliefs

grey to a beautiful pink. They were awfully small but they were delicious.

The whole week I felt as though I were in heaven. I caught shrimps, waded in the tidal pools, and ate saffron buns, Cornish pasties and strawberries with clotted Cornish cream on top. One day my father took me to the fishing docks where the fishermen were mending their nets. He sat down and talked to them, but I couldn't understand a word of what they said.

"They're speaking Cornish," my father told me. "It's an old language and very few people speak it any more. I understand it because I was a child in Cornwall. It makes me think of my own childhood when I talk to the fishermen."

My father stopped talking and winked at me.

"I was just teasing. They weren't speaking Cornish at all. But they speak English with such a funny accent it sounds like a different language entirely."

I decided that I didn't want to talk to any fishermen after that. If I couldn't understand what they were saying to me I would just be embarrassed.

There were no air raid sirens in St. Ives and I hardly even thought about the war. I just wanted to stay there forever. But after a week we had to go back to Reading. They needed my father at Thorneycroft's. I returned to Reading with happy memories and a terrible sunburn.

Beliefs

Shortly after we returned from St. Ives the Battle of Britain began. The Germans began bombing our airfields and factories. Spitfires and Hurricanes took to the air to battle the German bombers and the Me-109s that escorted them. If the Germans won supremacy of the air they would be able to begin their invasion of Britain. What if they decided to bomb Thorneycroft's? My father would be killed.

Once again Winston Churchill inspired us with a radio speech.

"Let us all strive without failing in faith or in duty, and the dark curse of Hitler will be lifted from our age."

I believed in Churchill's words with all my heart. Faith. Duty. We were all part of a great crusade against evil. Hitler had conquered Czechoslovakia, Poland, Denmark, Norway Holland, Belgium and France. Now it was up to us to stand up to him or else he would conquer the rest of the world. It was on our shoulders. If only I were old enough to fly a Spitfire.

But my parents had less heroic ideas that they had hatched in the dark nights in our slug-infested shelter. My mother was to take Elizabeth and me to Canada.

*"No, no, no,"* I thought. *"That's not what's supposed to happen. We're supposed to stay here and fight the Germans just as Churchill wants. It's cowardly to run away."*

Beliefs

*6: Away to Canada*

But I couldn't say it. The decision had been made. I was only eight years old and it was up to my parents to make those kinds of decisions. But I was old enough to believe fervently

Beliefs

that, no matter how well-intentioned my parents were, they were wrong.

With a heavy heart I said goodbye to my friend, Freddy Price, and promised to write to him. He promised to write back, but I could tell by the expression on his face that he too thought it was wrong for me to escape to Canada.

"You'll have to say goodbye to David Walker too," my mother announced.

David wasn't a school friend. He was a friend that my mother had chosen for me because she and Mrs. Walker were friends. David didn't go to school and the only way he could have friends was if his mother invited friends to come to their house. The reason for all that was David was an invalid. He had something called an aneurysm that meant that he could die at any moment. So when I went to David's place I wasn't allowed to roughhouse with him. I could play with his model trains or his toy soldiers or trade stamps with him but I wasn't allowed to wrestle in case I accidentally killed him. It was a heavy responsibility.

But it was still fun visiting with David. His parents were rich and they lived in a huge mansion with beautiful grounds. If I went there in the afternoon, Mrs. Walker liked to appear halfway through playtime with a silver tray covered with biscuits and sweets. Mrs. Walker was a friend of an Anglican clergyman named Canon Rowe. Canon Rowe was a bald man with a jolly laugh. He always brought postage stamps from all over the world and taught David and me how to start a stamp collection. He made me feel good because by being with him I learned that not all Anglicans were running around persecuting Catholics. I didn't think that Canon Rowe would be capable of persecuting anyone.

"Goodbye, David," I said. "I have to go to Canada. But I will write you letters and when the war is over we can get together and be friends again."

"Of course," David replied. "We can get together again and nothing will have changed."

But in my heart of hearts I wondered if David would still be alive. He was so frail and if a bomb dropped even close to him... I had to put that thought out of my mind and hope for the best.

## CHAPTER 4

# ON BEING HIP

When I had said my goodbyes, my mother bundled Elizabeth and myself into the night train from Reading to Liverpool. When we reached Liverpool in the morning we scurried from the station to the docks where our ship was waiting. It was called the *Duchess of Athol*.

The first part of the trip was boring, nerve-wracking and uncomfortable all at the same time. We had to wear our life jackets day and night in case a German U-boat decided to torpedo us. The weather was rough so we had to spend most of our time in a tiny stateroom with a single porthole. There was nothing to look at though. Just waves.

The only good thing about our stateroom was that I got to sleep in the upper bunk. Elizabeth had to sleep with our mother in the lower bunk..

My mother tried to cheer me up. "There's a nickname for this ship," she said. "It's called *The Drunken Duchess*."

I knew that was supposed to be a joke but I didn't think it was funny. All I knew was that I was seasick and I couldn't eat. The worst part of it was worrying about U-boats. I

## On Being Hip

would rather have been back in Reading waving a pitchfork at the German army if they decided to invade. But what could I do against a U-boat? They traveled underwater and fired torpedoes. I wouldn't know if one was there until the ship blew up and I was hurled into the cold water.

And then I had this terrible feeling of running away. My father was still back in Reading and going to Thorneycroft's Shipyard every day. He could be bombed. My schoolmates would be going back to school in a week or two and I wouldn't be there with them. If they had to fight off the Germans I wouldn't be able to help. I was an evacuee. Something like the Delaney brothers except that I was leaving England altogether. I was angry with my parents for making this choice about my life and angry with myself. I saw myself as a coward and a deserter.

I spent the first few days feeling sick and brooding about going to Canada. Then suddenly everything improved. The captain announced on a loudspeaker that we were out of U-boat range and that we could come up onto the deck without our life jackets.

What a glorious sight! The sun was out and the wind had died down. All around us were the other ships in our convoy. Our destroyer escorts had left. Assured that our ships were now safe they had turned around and headed back to England. But why, I wondered, were they doing a stupid job like escorting evacuees to Canada when they should be sinking German ships somewhere?

"Would you like to fight?"

I couldn't believe it. The challenge had come from a girl, a tall angular girl in a school uniform.

"How old are you?" I asked..

"Nine."

I was still only eight, and she was a two or three inches taller than I was. Taking into consideration the fact that she was a girl it would be a fair fight. But I was puzzled.

I had never heard of girls fighting or even wanting to fight.

"Fist fight or wrestling?"

"Fist fight."

We feinted a few times and then I let my guard down. I did not believe that a girl was capable of hitting me.

Sock! Crack!

She not only hit me, but she hit me square in the mouth. It was one of my teeth that had made the cracking sound. After that I really went after her.

"Had enough now?" I asked. I was all out of breath. I wanted to stop but I wanted to make it appear as though she was the one giving in

"Yes."

"Fair fight?"

"Yes, fair. Even?"

"Even."

She walked away and back to her stateroom. It was the first time in my life that a girl had paid any attention to me. When I went back to my stateroom I looked into the mirror. She had knocked a small chip away from the corner of one of my front teeth. If anyone were to ask me about it, I could say that I had been in a fight. I wouldn't have wanted to tell anyone that a girl had done the damage.

The warm sunny weather didn't last very long. It turned cold and foggy as we approached Canada.

"If you go up onto the deck now you can see an iceberg off the starboard bow. We will be passing fairly close to it. This may be the first time that any of you has ever seen an iceberg."

The captain's announcement sent us running up to the passenger deck. The iceberg was larger than I could have imagined. I had read somewhere that the largest part of an iceberg lay underwater so it must have been huge. I had also read about how the Titanic had been sunk by an iceberg, but I could tell that our captain wasn't taking any chances. He reduced speed and steered past it carefully. Then we ran back to our staterooms. It was much too cold standing on the deck.

It wasn't long before we were back in warm, sunny weather again. When the captain called us up to the passenger deck again it was for our first sight of land.

"That's the province of Nova Scotia ahead and slightly to starboard. We should be in the port of Halifax in a few hours."

We soon glided into port. The first thing we saw was a huge sign above the dock. It read,

> PIER 21. WELCOME TO CANADA

My mother was overjoyed.

"Home at last!"

Home to her perhaps, but not to me. England was my home, but I was really glad to get off the boat. When I walked onto the dock I swayed uncertainly from side to side. I was walking as though I were still on the ship.

"Sea legs," my mother informed me. "It's because you've been walking back and forth on a ship and now you're standing on something that isn't moving. You'll get over it very quickly."

After we had passed through the customs shed we were greeted by my mother's sister, Auntie Bea, and her two children, Marjorie and David. Auntie Bea was warm and friendly. Marjorie and David were both older than me. They didn't look all that thrilled to be meeting us.

"Wait until you see Joanne," Auntie Bea said. "She's the most adorable little thing you've ever seen in your life. She's at home right now with her Amah."

"I can hardly wait," my mother replied. "You told us all about her in your letter."

We all trooped off to the Naval Dockyard. Auntie Bea's husband, Uncle Roy, was a Commander in the Royal Canadian Navy, and had three gold stripes on the sleeves of his uniform so that everyone could see his rank. We were to stay with Uncle Roy, Auntie Bea, Marjorie, David and Joanne until we could find a place of our own or until the war was over. I didn't really know which might come first. All I knew for sure was that I was being forced to live in someone else's home just so I wouldn't get bombed.

When we reached the Dockyard I found out what an Amah was. She was a Chinese lady who had been hired to look after Joanne while Auntie Bea was busy doing things. I took a quick look at Joanne. All I could see was a tiny pink creature wrapped up in white woolens. Even less interesting than my sister.

I didn't like the look of the Naval Dockyard. It was a mixture of old brick buildings and newer buildings that were painted grey. There were several naval ships docked in the harbour and seamen walking unevenly up and down narrow cobblestone streets.

I looked around to see if there were any gardens but there were none.

I felt homesick for Sunny Corner.

My cousin David was three and a half years my senior. He chewed gum, combed a wave into his blond hair and knew just about everything there was to know about movie stars, comics and songs.

"Okay, let's see your comic books."

I fumbled around in the bottom of my suitcase and pulled out the tattered remains of my *Beano Comics*.

"What's this? Do you call these comics? They're not even in colour. Don't you have any Superman?

I shook my head.

"Here's Superman." David went to a shelf and pulled out the latest edition of *Action Comics*.

"Haven't you heard of Superman? He's the strongest man in the world. So get hip. Okay?"

Get hip? I had never heard that expression before, but the meaning was perfectly clear.

## On Being Hip

I had to start thinking and talking like a Canadian whether I liked it or not. And "okay"? That was slang and I wouldn't have dared to speak like that in my mother's presence.

"And look. Here's Captain Marvel and here's Batman. They're okay but not near as strong as Superman. And Batman has to have that kid Robin along with him to get anything done."

That *kid* Robin? More slang. I would just have to get used to it.

"What songs do you like?"

"I don't know many songs but l always like it when George Formby sings the song about cleaning windows and Gracie Fields has a funny song about an aspidistra."

I was hoping to impress David but he looked at me as though I had arrived from a different planet. Which in a sense I had.

"A song about a what? Oh never mind. Nobody's ever heard of those people anyway. Have you heard of Glenn Miller? Or Benny Goodman? Or Duke Ellington?"

I stared at David dumbfounded and shook my head. I had never heard of any of them.

"No? Well you'd better get hip then. You don't want people thinking you're some dumb limey, do you? Here's some songs you'd better learn. Ready?"

## On Being Hip

"Mairzy Doats and doatzy doats and little lambs eat ivy..."

"Hutsut Ralston on a rillerra and a brawla brawla suet..."

I listened intently taking in every word. Before long I'd learned all the words to the Hutsut Song, Mairzy Doats and Three Little Fishies. None of the words in Mairzy Doats or the Hutsut Song made any sense. But they didn't need to. The important thing for me was to learn all the words and learn them fast so I would be hip.

"Here's some rhymes for you to learn," David continued.

"Hoity-toity

Sitting on a coibstone

Eatin' woims and boipin'

Along comes goil-friend Moitle...."

"One bright morning in the middle of the night

Two dead boys got up to fight..."

And on and on it went. Next came the movie stars. The only movies I had ever seen in my life were *Snow White* and *The Wizard of Oz*. They had both scared the wits out of me but they had happy endings.

## On Being Hip

"Have you seen any of the Abbot and Costello movies? Bob Hope? Bing Crosby? *The Road to Zanzibar*? Any of the *Road* movies?

"No, I haven't." I shook my head sadly.

"And now....hubba...hubba...hubba...for the glamour girls. Have you heard of Rita Hayworth? Dorothy Lamour? Hedy Lamarr? Veronica Lake? Marlene Dietrich?"

"No. Why are they called grammar girls?"

David collapsed with laughter.

"Glamour girls. Not grammar girls, stupid."

David got away with a lot. Whenever Uncle Roy or Auntie Bea tried to correct his behaviour he came out with a funny one-line quip. They were never really able to put him in his place. I tried to copy David and come out with some quips of my own. They never quite worked and each time I failed David would give me a scornful look. He obviously thought that I was an inconsequential little English grub.

After a few days I was liking Halifax a little better. There were always warships to watch coming in and out of the harbour and when the adults weren't too busy we were taken to a beach where there were rocky outcrops covered with blueberry bushes. I had never seen blueberries before and I quickly developed a passion for them. I was even

## On Being Hip

starting to feel a little more hip. Not as hip as David of course but I was learning.

It was Auntie Bea's birthday so David and I set out for downtown Halifax so he could buy her a box of chocolates. The storekeeper carefully gift-wrapped them. I was drooling because we hadn't had chocolates in England. Sugar was rationed and all the Cadbury's chocolates had disappeared from the shops. We were halfway down Barrington Street walking back to the Dockyard when two street urchins came running out of an alley, knocked David to the ground and made off with his chocolates. My first thought was that the Delaney boys had followed us to Canada but it wasn't them. It was two other boys who were just as tough and just as nasty.

David arrived home in tears and minus the chocolates. That was the last of his allowance and he had no way of buying another present. For the rest of the day David was in mourning. I liked him a lot better when I found out that he could be soft and tearful as well as hip and funny.

The following day there was news. Uncle Roy had been promoted from being a Commander to being a Commodore in charge of Canada's Pacific Fleet. Commodore Beech. We had to pack up and leave for Victoria, British Columbia. We had been in Halifax for only one month.

CHAPTER *5*

# RETURN TO VICTORIA

I didn't want to leave Halifax. I had just got settled and I wanted to pick more blueberries. But we had to leave, and this time we were to cross the continent all the way to Victoria. My mother couldn't have been happier. The rest of her family was in Victoria. Victoria was where I had been born and spent the first four years of my life.

I couldn't really remember it. I had a vague image of flowers, chickens, pebbly beaches and my grandfather, a kindly man who liked to watch me while I played. That was all. I might as well have been going to a foreign country. And what about my father? He would be on the opposite side of the world from us and I wondered if I would ever see him again.

Uncle Roy was expected to move to Victoria immediately and that meant we had to pack quickly. We boarded the train in Halifax. The train was a lot of fun. It was much bigger than the English trains and it had a dining car where we could sit around a table to eat dinner. At nighttime I had my own bunk to sleep in. The sheets were crisp and white and felt cool to the touch. I felt really grown up climbing up the ladder to my bunk.. Elizabeth wasn't allowed up there. She had to sleep in the lower bunk with my mother.

## Return to Victoria

In the morning my mother called me to look out the window. There was a huge building towering over us.

"That's the Chateau Frontenac," my mother informed me. "We're in Quebec City."

I don't really remember much after that. Going through Ontario and the Prairies was really boring. First it was endless forest and then endless prairies. The novelty of being on a train wore off quickly. I felt off balance the whole time. It was difficult walking from our carriage to the dining car without swaying and bumping into people.

My mother kept me entertained with an old photograph album. There were a lot of photographs of me before we left Victoria for England. The first four years of my life. There were photographs of me sniffing flowers, chasing chickens, picking up stones on the beach and sitting beside my grandfather. There was nothing there that I could really remember, and I didn't like the fact that I was dressed in a little white suit and sunhat in all of them. I thought I looked like a sissy, but my mother said I looked adorable.

"Look," she said. "There you are in the garden. You loved flowers. And there you are feeding the chickens. Do you remember when that big rooster chased you around the farm? And there you are shaking earwigs from the dahlias into a big bucket filled with water. Your grandfather would give you a peppermint for drowning all those earwigs. Do you remember picking up those big rocks from the beach?

You used to say *hebby* for heavy. And there you are playing with your little friend Cameron? Do you remember how Cameron used to call his toy car a "car-car"? And how you corrected him by calling it a car?"

*"What a silly little twerp I must have been,"* I thought, but I didn't say anything. My mother was obviously enjoying this and I didn't want to hurt her feelings. The truth was that I didn't remember any of it, but the next time I looked at the album it felt as though I were remembering some of it. Most probably I was just remembering looking at the photographs.

I determined that when we got to Victoria I wasn't going to do any sissy stuff like sniffing flowers and running around after chickens. I was much too grown up for that kind of thing. But I did want to see my grandfather.

When we reached the Rocky Mountains my mother put the album away and told me to look out the window. I was amazed at what I saw. I had seen pictures of mountains before but never imagined that they would be so high. For some reason I felt frightened just as though I were standing at the top of a tall building instead of at the base of the mountains. It felt as though I were going to fall even though there was nowhere to fall except up.

No sooner had I overcome this uncomfortable feeling when something else happened to frighten me. The train made a long piercing whistle and then disappeared into a tunnel.

## Return to Victoria

The tunnel went on and on and then I was afraid that we would never come out into daylight again. It was a great relief to me when we finally left the tunnels and mountains and leveled out in the softer green valleys of British Columbia.

We finally reached Vancouver and then boarded a ship for Victoria. It was beginning to seem as though the succession of ships and trains would never end. But it did. The Beech family had arrived just ahead of us and were there to greet us. Then they took us to our final destination, the big Naval Dockyard in Esquimalt.

I didn't like the look of the Dockyard. We passed several grim-looking brick buildings with shuttered windows. One of them had the word *STORE* painted on the side in big block letters. The building didn't look like any store I had ever seen before. There was nothing to buy there. To me it was just another grim brick building. Finally we reached a huge red brick house that faced onto the water.

"Home at last," Auntie Bea announced in her chirpiest voice.

She was so cheerful and she made it sound as though she had been living there forever instead of just for a day or two. It didn't seem to me like any home I could think of. It was much too big. It didn't have the cozy feeling of our home at Sunny Corner.

"I'll show you all to your rooms," she continued, as she led us upstairs. "Here, John, you will sleep in the big bedroom with David. By the way this is called the Admirals House, even though your Uncle Roy is only a commodore."

Only a commodore? It seemed to me that Auntie Bea was being a little too modest. I had already seen Uncle Roy's new uniform with four stripes on each sleeve. He was in charge of everything here. She led me into an enormous room with high ceilings and windows that looked out to sea. There were two cots set far apart from each other.

7: Uncle Roy

"Lots of space so you don't bump into one another. And there's a bathroom just outside in the hallway. Your windows look right out onto the Strait of Juan de Fuca. Today's a nice day so you can see the Olympic Mountains in Washington."

I didn't care about the view. I just wanted a cozy little room to myself. I didn't want to share a room with David. He didn't think I was hip and he would just make fun of me when no-one else was listening. More wisecracks, songs, glamour girls and a whole bunch of things that didn't really interest me. I had hoped to be able to see the naval ships just like I had in Halifax but the red brick buildings that lined the road into our new home formed a barrier. I wasn't even allowed to walk down to where the ships were lying at anchor without being "out of bounds". Everything surrounding the naval ships was secret and hush-hush.

There was no time for me to sit around and brood though. Summer had come to an end and the next day I was to start attending my new school.

*8: The backyard, Admirals House*

## CHAPTER 6

# GLENLYON

On the first day of school I set out on my own. I had asked my mother to write out the directions for me. I was afraid that, if she went with me on the first day, the other boys would make fun of me. The first thing I had to do was to board the Esquimalt streetcar at the entrance to the Dockyard. Then I had to ask for a transfer and ask the conductor to let me off at the corner of Douglas and Yates. At my transfer point I had to find out where the Oak Bay streetcar stopped, get on and ask the conductor to let me off at the very end of Oak Bay Avenue. After that it was easy. All I had to do was walk along Prospect Place and San Carlos Avenue down to Beach Drive, and there was my new school right in front of me. It looked more like a rich person's mansion than a school.

Glenlyon Preparatory School. My mother had dressed me exactly right. Grey flannel shorts, a grey flannel jacket, an itchy grey shirt, a tie with horizontal blue and white stripes, shiny black shoes and a cap with badge that showed a lion standing on its hind legs. Except for the setting everything looked exactly like the school I had left behind me in Reading.

My new headmaster came out and after he had rung a large bell we assembled on the tarmac in front of the school. His name was Mr. Simpson. He had a wide moustache, pressed grey pants and a heavy brown tweed jacket that looked like a tailored doormat

He ordered us to form two lines and stand at attention. Then he raised the flag. First he led us in singing *God Save the King* and then *O Canada*. I didn't know the words to *O Canada*, but once I figured out that *true patriot love* wasn't all one word I found it easy to learn. Then we said the Lord's Prayer and I remembered not to say the Anglican add-on words out loud.

"Hold out yerrr hands, boys." Mr. Simpson had come to Canada from Scotland and when he said the word *your* he made the "r" into a long rolling sound.

We held out our hands while Mr. Simpson inspected them topside and underside. There was to be no dirt wedged under our fingernails. Then he inspected our shoes. They were to be shined to perfection. No scuff marks were permitted. Our hair was to be brushed and parted in a straight line.

"How many of ye will be coming to school on the streetcar?"

Several of us raised our hands.

"Remember that if an adult enters the streetcar and there are no seats available, ye're to stand up and offer yerrr seat immediately. Ye represent yerrr school whenever ye're in public. And if ye're sitting there comfortably don't turn yerrr minds to idle thoughts. Think of our brave young men in uniform who risk their lives every day fighting the Hun just so ye can be safe and comfortable."

I could feel hotness creeping up the back of my neck. I felt ashamed. Here I was warm and comfortable when I should have been in England with those brave young men, not sitting out the war here in Canada.

Mr. Simpson went on to explain how we were to conduct ourselves in school. We were allowed to wrestle as long as it was with a boy our own size, but we were not allowed to use our fists. As I already had a chipped tooth from my encounter on the *Duchess of Athol* I thought that was a sensible rule. If we had broken a rule we were expected to own up. If we knew of another boy who had broken a rule we were not to snitch. When we were playing games we were expected to "play fair"- unlike those Nazi bullies who didn't understand fair play. There was only one word to remember and that was "sportsmanship". Except for the fistfighting rule it was pretty much the same as Reading Grammar School. I understood exactly what was expected.

As one of the youngest boys in the school I was assigned to Form One. My new teacher was Mr. Upward. He was young and seemed friendly enough. He wore a checkered sports coat, had a wave in his hair and spoke in a familiar reassuring English accent. At the end of our first day he handed us a list of school supplies. The following day we were expected to turn up with a sharpened pencil, a ruler, an eraser, a fine nib pen, extra nibs and gym supplies.

The journey home on the streetcar took over an hour and by the time I had returned to the Admirals House the sun was already setting.

Once I had memorized the route from the Dockyard to Glenlyon I found plenty to occupy myself. Waiting for the streetcar to arrive at the Dockyard gate in the morning gave me time to look for the *Sweet Caporal* cigarette packages that sailors had thrown by the wayside. Each package was a prize that had a drawing of a British, German, French or Italian warplane on the cover. I tried to collect the whole set and if I had a duplicate I could trade with one of the other boys. Inside the package there was *silver paper* which had been placed there to keep the cigarettes moist. Once on the streetcar I carefully folded the paper into pellets. They had to be exactly the right size and shape to shoot at the other boys with elastics when Mr. Upward, or "Uppie" as we called him, had his back turned.

The streetcar itself had leaflets called "The Buzzer" which we were allowed to take. The Buzzer always had a picture of an animated bolt of electricity called "Reddy Kilowatt" on the front. It was an advertisement put out by B.C. Electric Railway Company telling us how great a company they were. Inside the Buzzer were boring announcements about changes in service. The Buzzer could be ripped and folded into strips and then folded again into pellets. They weren't nearly as good as silver paper but they were useful as a backup.

When I transferred at Douglas and Yates I had a second chance to look for *Sweet Caporal* packages. It was more difficult there because there were street cleaners in the middle of town who swept up litter.

Once I arrived at my final stop there were more opportunities for mischief. There was a path and steps that led down to Beach Drive. Along the path there was speargrass growing. If I chose to walk that route I could grab a handful, stuff them in my pocket and when the opportunity presented itself I could throw a spear into another boy's woolen sock. They were difficult to extricate and caused an uncomfortable itch. Or if my chosen victim had taken off his jacket and was sitting there wearing just a grey pullover, I could aim a spear at his back. If it landed square between his shoulder blades he would find it difficult to pull out. Of course I had to expect retaliation when my guard was down.

When I got bored with speargrass there was another grass with tough wide blades I could collect. I had to be careful tearing the grass away from the plant because I could cut my fingers on the sharp blades. Once I had a piece the right length and width I could place it between my thumbs and blow into it. If the grass was tight I could make a shrill whistling sound, and then, if I loosened it a little I could make a farting sound that was sure to get a laugh from the other boys.

In September I approached the school from Prospect Place and San Carlos Avenue and collected the chestnuts that had dropped during the night. The best ones were still partly hidden in their green casings. They were still cool in the early morning and I pulled them out of their casings and pressed them against my cheeks. Aaah! All the boys collected chestnuts and dried them out for *conker* contests. They drilled holes in their dried-out chestnuts, ran a string through them, and then they were ready for a contest. Then they took turns aiming their conkers at their opponent's conkers. The boy who cracked another boy's conker in half was declared a winner. A really tough conker might win its owner several contests before it finally cracked. The other boys were able to dry out their chestnuts quickly by slipping them into their mothers' ovens. I couldn't do that because the kitchen at the Admirals House was "out of bounds". I had to be patient and let them dry naturally.

In addition to having my pockets stuffed with conkers, pellets, elastics, speargrass and blades of grass, I had a small bag of marbles. My best marbles had a red or yellow spiral embedded in the glass, but they were hard to get because of the war. Most of the time we had to put up with marbles that were a murky mixture of green, blue and brown. The worst marbles were called "doughboys". They were made of baked clay and painted. They cracked almost as easily as our conkers did. The very best were the "steelies". These were ball bearings that had been purloined from one of the shipyards. They had to be the right size. The small ones were practically useless. The big ones were impressive but impractical, but if you were lucky enough to have one just the right size you had an unbeatable shooter. I felt guilty when I had a steelie in my possession because they were supposed to be important to the War Effort.

To play marbles you drew a circle in the dirt, put your marbles inside the circle, and then began by shooting from outside the circle. The boys who were really good at it knew just how to place a spin on their shooters so that they stayed exactly in place after hitting a marble out of the ring. If you knocked a marble out of the ring you were allowed to keep it. Try as I might I never learned how to place a spin on my shooter. Because I had to kneel to play marbles my knees were dirty and bleeding much of the time. This annoyed my mother who had to remove the gravel from my knees with a washcloth before she applied boracic acid and iodine.

"For goodness sakes. Stay off your knees or you'll wear them out altogether," my mother said. "And don't keep picking at your scabs. You'll get an infection and anyway it's disgusting."

I listened to my mother politely but I never changed my behaviour. How could I possibly play marbles without getting down onto my knees?

Glenlyon School had been built on the waterfront right above Oak Bay Beach. At one end of the property Bowker Creek flowed into the sea. It was the perfect setting for my favourite subject – Nature Study. Uppie took us out on fine days and taught us to identify the great variety of ducks and shorebirds. There were mallards, widgeons, grebes, coots, killdeer, sandpipers, mergansers, gulls, terns, scoters, teal, bufflehead, wood ducks, pintails and cormorants.

"I expect you to be able to tell the difference between the western grebe and the merganser. They're about the same size, they have the same diving habits, but as you can see, the merganser has a copper-coloured head with feathers sticking straight out at the back."

It was easy and fun, just like recognizing the difference between Spitfires and Hurricanes. Uppie became my hero because he introduced me to the natural world in my new home. On fine days he took us to the beach in front of the school, and if he was in a good mood, he would take us all the way to Cattle Point in the Uplands and test our identification skills there.

Uppie also taught History and Geography and something called Current Events. The classroom had a map of the world that unrolled like a blind. At the bottom of the map was a huge picture of a Neilson's chocolate bar. All the countries of the British Empire were coloured pink. Half the world was British. By comparison Hitler's Europe was tiny. How could Hitler expect to win the war with all those huge countries – Canada, Australia, India and half of Africa – lined up against him? He didn't have a chance.

Uppie expected us to read the Victoria Colonist and listen to the BBC News every evening so we would know what was happening in the war. I followed the war avidly and every day I knew the exact toll of enemy planes compared with the number of planes lost by the brave pilots of the Royal Air Force.

I listened as though my life depended on it, which indeed it did. At recess we rushed onto the playground with the latest news about the Battle of Britain. Once on the playground we were Spitfires and Hurricanes shooting down the bombers of Goering's Luftwaffe. London was in flames but with each passing day the toll of enemy bombers rose. By October it seemed that Great Britain had prevailed and that the Germans had abandoned their invasion plans.

I was filled with Churchill's words: "Never in the field of human conflict was so much owed by so many to so few. All hearts go out to the fighter pilots."

My heart went out too, but it was heavy. I could have been there in England celebrating the victories in the air, but instead I was thousands of miles away. Sitting out the war in Canada while history was being made at home.

With thoughts about the war stirring my imagination it was difficult to concentrate on a boring subject like Arithmetic. Simmie taught us Arithmetic. When I faltered with the nine times table he bellowed at me.

"All ye do is add up the digits, and if the digits add up to nine, ye know that the number is a product of nine times something. Now pay attention, ye rubbishy fellow or I'll put ye in my pocket."

Simmie seemed so large and imposing I could almost believe it would be possible for him to pick me up and put me in his pocket. I learned the nine times table and never forgot it.

Mr. Turpin taught English Grammar and Composition. Mr. Turpin was a lean man with wire-rimmed glasses and a sleeveless jersey that always seemed on the verge of coming unravelled. He taught Grammar from a green book written by two gentlemen named McLaurin and Campbell. At the end of every chapter were several sentences that were meant to illustrate the use of various parts of speech. We were supposed to be able to recognize the part of speech according to the way it was used in a sentence. In the sentence "He sent in orders for books", for example, the word *orders* was a noun, but that in the sentence "The colonel orders his troops to stand at attention", the word *orders* was a verb. If you were unable to make that distinction Mr. Turpin had a way of looking at you through his wire-rimmed glasses that made you feel quite stupid. I liked Grammar because it all seemed to make sense and I found it easy. I loved English Composition because no matter what the topic was I was able to use my imagination. If Mr. Turpin thought I had written something worthwhile, he would read it aloud to the class.

Apart from Arithmetic the only subject I didn't like was Music. A woman whose name I forget came to the school once a week to teach us. We had to stand to sing and she banged on the piano until my ears hurt. She played *"There'll Always Be an England"* and we sang our hearts out because we were thinking of the Battle of Britain and the Blitz. We sang *"Rule Britannia"* and knew in our hearts that, whatever Hitler tried next, he would be defeated by the gallant British Navy. And then, when she felt that we needed a rest from these patriotic outbursts, she led us in singing *"Loch Lomond"*.

*"By yon bonnie banks and by yon bonnie braes? What a sappy song!"* I thought. *"Who could possibly care about some place in Scotland with bonnie banks?"* I suspected that *"Loch Lomond"* was Simmie's idea.

After school we had games. In September games consisted of soccer. We had to walk all the way to Windsor Park to play in the grass and mud. If it was pouring rain we went inside *The Boathouse* at the back of the school. It wasn't used for storing boats but there was enough room for Uppie to set up mats and horses so we could learn gymnastics. I was a little too small to jump up onto the horse with any degree of ease, and I usually felt sore and bruised at the end of a session. Then if Uppie decided we needed a change of pace he would have us run all the way to Cattle Point and back. The run was called "Cross Country". By the time I had turned around and headed back to the school I had a stitch in my side and couldn't run at all. I usually came in last or close to last. After games I still had at least an hour ahead of me before finally getting home on the streetcar.

Recess was when I got to know the other boys and to make friends. I liked Richard Preston because he was even-tempered. Even if he lost at marbles he would take it all in his stride and not get mad. I liked Donald Carmichael because he was almost as small as I was and liked to wrestle. I could always count on him for an even match. I liked Rene Desjarlais because his father owned a doughnut shop on Douglas Street really close to where I transferred from one streetcar to another. If I came by at the right time I could expect to be treated with one of the round balls that were left over after the doughnut machine had punched holes into the doughnuts.

Jeremy Carrington was fun because he had learned all the Churchill speeches by heart. When we played war games he always got to be Churchill and shouted out things like "We will fight them on the beaches".

I was afraid of Cameron McLoughlin. He had a dramatic way of dominating the playground just by looking tough. None of us ever thought of crossing or challenging him.

War games were the best fun. When we weren't being Spitfires or Hurricanes or Me-109s we were British Commandos, German storm troopers or Gestapo agents. I had Brylcreemed black hair that I flattened and a black comb that I pushed against my upper lip when I was pretending to be Hitler.

"Take zeez prisoners to zeir cells and make zem talk. Ja, give zem ze acid bath. Zen zey vill talk. Don't chust stand zere, dumbkopf. Moof!"

There was one thing I had to learn to be fully accepted by the other boys, and that was to drop my English accent. I thought that was odd because Uppie had an English accent and Mr. Turpin had an English accent, but of course they were adults and didn't really count.

"Come on Hemy. Don't talk like a limey."

I found it hard to drop my accent, but I kept working at it. The other thing I got teased about was being small. That earned me the nickname of "Twerp". I had a habit of blinking when I was nervous and that earned me the nickname of "Blinky". And finally, I had a habit of daydreaming during Grammar classes. That earned me the nickname of "Sleepy". Sometimes I wished I were back at Reading Grammar School where I had Freddy Price for a friend and didn't have to worry about my accent.

Lunch at school was an ordeal. Lunches were prepared and served by Mrs. Simpson, the headmaster's wife. We called her "Matron". She was a Presbyterian lady who combed her straight hair back into a bun. She believed in plain food, and served us tasteless desserts like blancmange that invariably had lumps in them. It was all I could do to get through lunch without gagging.

One day when we were struggling with our chocolate puddings I noticed Donald Carmichael taking a particularly large mouthful. One of the other boys noticed too and in a low voice made a funny remark about the pudding. Donald wanted to laugh but he couldn't with his mouth full. He pursed his lips tight and then his mouthful of pudding squirted out through his nostrils and all over the dining room table. It was a disgusting sight but we didn't care. Once we were safely away from the dining room and onto the school grounds we burst into gales of laughter.

Most of the time I liked school. The masters were fair and it was fun playing war games with the other boys. Eventually I lost most of my English accent.

The other requirement for belonging was exactly the same at Glenlyon as it had been at Reading Grammar School. I had to be caned by the headmaster at least once. I cannot remember exactly what I did to earn this privilege. I may have hit one of the other boys in the back of the neck with a silver paper pellet with enough force to cause him to cry out, but I'm not really sure. It may have been something else. In any event Simmie summoned me to his study. It was called the "Sun-Room" and had a marvelous view of the grounds, the sea and the islands beyond.

In one corner of the Sun-Room was an array of bamboo canes that he was supposed to have purchased from a Chinese market gardener. It was also believed in the school that he purchased a fresh lot every year as the dried out canes from the previous year were less springy.

"Hold out yerr hand, mon. No, higher than that, ye rubbishy fellow."

Simmie took a quick look at me and proceeded to select the shortest cane.

*"Thank goodness,"* I thought, *"he's going to hit my hand and not my bottom."*

Whack! Whack!

"Now yerr other hand."

Whack! Whack!

Four strokes. Twice the number administered by Mr. Peach the previous year, but only half the pain. Simmie had neither

Mr. Peach's deadly accuracy, nor the obvious delight Mr. Peach showed in inflicting pain.

"I don't want to see ye back here. Do ye understand? And don't stand there smirking, or I'll put ye in my pocket. Now get back to yerr classroom, ye rubbishy fellow."

And that was that. Just enough strokes so that I could go back to my classroom and boast about the experience.

## CHAPTER 7

# THE ADMIRALS HOUSE

<u>9</u>: *Admirals House*

I had a room in the Admirals House where I could play on the weekends. It was a large room in the basement with a bare wooden floor. It was a perfect place for my favourite toy, the Thunderbolt. The Thunderbolt was a Dinky Toy copy of the fastest racing car in the world. It had been clocked at almost 500 miles per hour on the Salt Lake Flats where all the top racing cars competed. My Thunderbolt was designed so that I could put my thumb on the hood and then

## The Admirals House

with a flick of the wrist send it racing across my playroom. It was fast!

My other toys were Dinky Toys that I had brought with me from England. I had English Tommies, German storm troopers and a few pieces of equipment like tanks, trucks and artillery. Just enough so I could stage a pretend war.

I enjoyed playing by myself and using my imagination but my mother decided I needed a friend. I couldn't invite any friends to come to the Admirals House because they wouldn't be allowed past the Dockyard gate. But I was allowed to leave the Dockyard and visit a friend, so my mother arranged for me to go over to Cameron McLoughlin's house. My mother and Cameron's mother were friends and, according to my mother, I had played "ever so nicely" with Cameron when we were both toddlers and before our family had moved to England.

However I was afraid of Cameron. He ruled the playground at school with his menacing looks. What would he be like at his home? The McLoughlin's home was on the Esquimalt waterfront with plenty of arbutus trees and rocks where we could play hide-and-go-seek.

Despite what my mother may have thought, Cameron wasn't one bit interested in playing "ever so nicely" Cameron's idea of play was to lure me close to the water, put a headlock on me, and threaten to throw me in the water. He was a bully. Then when Mrs. McLoughlin called us to lunch

75

I couldn't eat properly. I was too nervous to swallow the delicious food she had prepared for us, even when she coaxed me with a smile. She couldn't understand why I had such a poor appetite.

For some reason I never fought back when Cameron put a headlock on me. Perhaps I felt that fighting back was the wrong thing to do as a guest, or more likely I was afraid that I would lose and he would push me into the water. I never complained to Mrs. McLoughlin or my own mother. My mother had a high opinion of the McLoughlin family and probably wouldn't want to hear anything bad about them. And then if I told my mother that I was afraid of Cameron it would be like admitting that I was a coward, and I certainly didn't want to do that. Instead of doing anything to change the situation, I wrongly imagined that Cameron would get tired of doing headlocks and find an interesting game we could play instead. But he never did.

I didn't understand myself. All the time we were in England I imagined how brave I would be if the Germans attacked. Now here I was in Canada with an opportunity to be brave in a real situation, and I turned out to be a coward instead.

Then there was the matter of my faith. Before we left England my mother had promised my father that she would send me to Catholic Catechism every weekend. On Saturday morning she dutifully took me to a Catholic church in Esquimalt called "Our Lady, Queen of Peace" and left me there while she went off to do something more interesting. There were two rows of benches facing the altar. I sat there surrounded by the other children. They were punching each other, throwing spitballs and shouting. I didn't want their company. They were poorly dressed, noisy urchins with bad manners. A bit too much like the Delaney brothers for my liking. The Queen of Peace must have been looking the other way.

Father O'Malley entered, and the noise ended as he directed us to our Catechism books. I still had the one I had brought over from England with me. After a few minutes I became aware of an unpleasant smell. It was like cooked turnips. As Father O'Malley continued teaching and preaching the smell became worse. Then it dawned on me that the smell must be coming from Father O'Malley himself. He had bad breath – outrageously bad breath. It was nauseating. Was the man dying?

The next week I returned filled with the hope that perhaps Father O'Malley would have brushed his teeth or whatever he needed to do to improve his breath. No such luck. It was as bad as ever.

I made excuses to my mother on Saturday mornings. I wasn't feeling well. I had homework and so on. My mother accepted my excuses all too readily. She hadn't been too keen on sending me to a Catholic church in the first place.

Then I tried to worm my way out of going to Cameron's place.

"Mummy, I was wondering if I could go to Donald Carmichael's place instead this weekend. We have lots of fun together at school. You know, playing marbles and stuff like that."

My mother looked at me as though I had gone insane.

"Of course not. The Carmichaels have money but no breeding. Donald's father used to have a gas station before he won the Irish Sweepstakes. That's how Donald's parents can afford to send him to Glenlyon. You see enough of him at school as it is."

"Oh."

My ploy had failed but after that my visits to the McLoughlin home diminished. Perhaps my mother had come to the conclusion that I wasn't keen on the visits, or perhaps Mrs. McLoughlin was tired of watching me pick at her delicious lunches. Or perhaps she knew that her son was a problem and didn't quite know what to do with him. I never found out.

I celebrated my ninth birthday at the Admirals House. It couldn't have been better. I was given a B.B. gun and a card from my father telling me that I was old enough for a small gun but that I was to treat it with care. The other great present was a metal mold for making lead soldiers, a small amount of lead, and an iron ladle for melting the lead over an open flame.

I could hardly wait to try out my new gun. I raced down to the rocks below the Admirals House at low tide. I turned over some rocks and crabs came scuttling out with their claws poised for action.

Pow!

"Take that, Nazis!"

Soon the rocks were coated with the greenish-grey scum that crabs had inside them. It was revolting to look at so I stopped. Perhaps there were more exciting things I could do with my B.B. gun.

David had a B.B. gun too and he decided that having a live human target would be a lot more exciting than shooting crabs. One afternoon he spotted Marjorie walking down the garden path towards the rocks and fired a shot at her. He hit her right in the calf of her leg. She screamed out in pain and then ran after David. When she finally caught him she threw him to the ground and gave him a good pounding. By this time she had forgotten about the pain in her leg but was mad at David because the B.B. had made a run in her best stockings. I thought it was pretty nervy of David to have done such a thing.

I wouldn't have dared fire my gun at a living person, even a snooty teenager like Marjorie. Better to stick with crabs.

Making lead soldiers with my new metal mold was fun. I had enough firewood at my disposal to build a small fire in the fireplace of my "playroom". Then I put a chunk of lead into an iron ladle and melted it over the fire. It was fascinating watching the lead. After it melted it went red-hot and if I kept it over the fire long enough it went white-hot. Then I poured the molten lead into the mold, waited for it to cool and pried it apart with pen-knife. There like magic were two brand new shiny lead soldiers. My mother liked my new soldiers and let me paint some of them red with her nail polish.

I soon ran out of the lead that had come with the mold. Then one day when I was walking home from the Dockyard gate. I spotted a pile of lead bars at the side of the road. What good luck! If I took one would it be stealing? And was stealing a sin? Probably. And what about the War Effort? Surely every piece of lead was needed to help defeat Hitler.

I grabbed a bar anyway and hid it under my raincoat. No-one would miss one bar.

Once I had justified stealing one lead bar it was much easier to steal a second one. Especially as I hadn't been caught stealing the first one. The lead soldier army grew.

I was in the middle of melting a fresh bar of lead when my mother interrupted me.

"Come and listen to the BBC. Princess Elizabeth is going to speak."

"Yes, Mummy," I grumbled.

I liked listening to King George or Winston Churchill on the radio when they spoke, but the idea of listening to Princess Elizabeth seemed a bit much. How did she get to make a speech anyway? She was a child just like me. Older than me but a child nonetheless. And she was a girl into the bargain. But as soon as she started to speak I listened. She had a high, clear voice that caught my attention right away.

"All of us children who are still at home think continually of our friends and relations who have gone overseas – who have travelled thousands of miles to find a wartime home and a kindly welcome in Canada, Australia, New Zealand, South Africa and the United States of America."

By the time she finished speaking it felt as though she was tucking all the evacuee children into bed. But I didn't think she was speaking to me. She was speaking to all the children who had left England *without* their parents – not to sissies and cowards like me who had come to Canada with their mothers. I sulked. My parents could have sent Elizabeth and me to Canada on our own. Then we would have had something to be proud of. I could have gone to Fairbridge Farm School near Duncan. That was where the English children went who had come without their parents. I imagined them having a high old time feeding the goats and drinking real cream or whatever it was that children did on farms. Much better than being stuck here in the gloomy old Dockyard. And I wouldn't have been teased for having an English accent either. All the children at Fairbridge Farm had English accents.

"My! Isn't she wonderful! Such a fine young lady!" My mother was glowing with admiration.

We all admired the Royal Family. The Colonist ran photographs of them visiting people in the East End of London cheering them up after their homes had been blown to bits. But having Princess Elizabeth speaking on the radio came as a bit of a surprise. I thought it was a good idea, but she could have said something to children like Elizabeth and me who had been forced to come to Canada with their mothers. Just so we wouldn't feel left out.

Marjorie had been adopting superior airs after being hit with the B.B. and wrestling David to the ground. But it wasn't long before she got her come-uppance. There was a large aviary with several rare birds on the grounds at the Admirals House. It was Marjorie's job to fill the feeders and put down fresh papers every day. One day she forgot to close the door to the aviary after returning to the house. When Auntie Bea walked down to the aviary for a visit the birds had all flown away and were nowhere to be seen in the garden. It was the only time I ever saw Auntie Bea angry.

Marjorie was suitably shamed and stopped going around with her nose in the air.

There were wild birds on the property as well – pheasants and quail. Every so often Uncle Roy ordered Valentine, the head steward, to dispatch a few quail for dinner.

"Valentine, I think we'll have squab for dinner tonight."

"Yes sir."

Valentine stood at attention in his spotless white uniform, saluted Uncle Roy, then disappeared into the woods with a rifle. We heard rifle shots, and then at dinner he appeared with a large silver platter. When he lifted the cover there were a dozen steaming quail all roasted to a golden brown.

I loved watching the quail families running through the bushes on the Dockyard property, and hated to think of Valentine shooting them.

*"How terrible,"* I thought, *"to shoot all those poor birds just so we can stuff ourselves."*

But once I had finished my rather small share of the quail I was already looking forward to Valentine going out with his gun and shooting a few more.

One day we had a special celebration. One of Uncle Roy's officers, Commander Beard, had sailed a destroyer called the *Prince Robert* to the coast of Mexico, captured a German ship there, and made the crew prisoner before they had time to scuttle the ship. Then he made the crew sail it all the way to the Dockyard.

After the ship had sat in the drydock for several days we were allowed to see it and go onboard. It was the *Weser*, a harmless-looking merchant ship with concealed guns. We were actually allowed on board and could see where the guns were hidden. Then we were allowed to wander around and look at the officers' staterooms. Each stateroom was neat and tidy and each officer had a brass plate with his name on it. The only thing we didn't see was the officers. They had been taken away to a Prisoner of War camp.

*"Bloody Huns!"* I thought. *"Serves them right for starting the war."*

The other good thing about going to see the *Weser* was being allowed to walk through the Dockyard and see the drydocks where ships were being repaired or refitted. All the rest of the time this part of the Dockyard was out of bounds to civilians. The *Weser* was refitted as a Canadian ship, but I never got to see her flying the Canadian flag.

Seeing the *Weser* in the Dockyard made me feel better about living in Victoria. There really was a war going on and it was being fought right here in the Pacific as well as in Europe.

Uncle Roy was triumphant over the capture of the *Weser*.

"Valentine, we'll have roast pheasant for dinner this evening!"

The Admirals House

The pheasant was even better than quail. It had a lot more meat than quail and I left the table feeling warm and satisfied.

10: VR2008.21.109 MV Weser, German Supply Ship WW II

# CHAPTER 8

# CHRISTMAS IN VICTORIA

I wanted to see my grandparents. The last time I had seen them was in Esquimalt just before we left for England. I don't think I had a real memory of them but every so often my mother had brought out the photo album and showed me pictures of them. My favourite picture was of Grandpa sitting on a stool in the garden. He was smoking a pipe and watching me doing something with a bucket of water.

"Your grandpa always loved watching you," my mother explained. "You used to pull earwigs off the dahlias for him. There you are drowning the earwigs in a bucket of water."

There were other photos in the album. There were photos of where we had lived with my grandparents in the big house on Head Street. There was a photo of Grandma with my mother and me in a white wooly suit and a white hat. We all looked quite miserable.

"Did anyone else live in the big house?"

"Yes. There was a lady named Annie who used to do the washing for us. Sometimes when she was finished she would read you a story. You were very fond of her. Then early each morning the Chinaman came all the way from Chinatown to start the furnace. Then he stayed and did chores but he didn't live with us."

"What about Daddy?"

"He was living in Nelson most of the time. He had to work in a garage to make money so we could eat. It was during the Depression and jobs were hard to find."

"Oh!"

I thought about my grandparents. Grandpa Wolfenden smoked a pipe and was kind to me. Grandma Wolfenden looked after the big house and looked sad all the time. That was about all I knew.

"Mummy, can we visit the house on Head Street?"

"No. Grandma had to move after Grandpa died."

"He's dead? Nobody told me."

"I told you on the train when I was showing you the photograph album? I told you he had passed away. Weren't you paying attention?"

## Christmas in Victoria

I guess I hadn't quite accepted that he was dead and if we went to Head Street we would see him there sitting in the garden.

"How did he die?"

"He got sick from smoking his pipe so much."

That was obviously all my mother wanted to tell me.

"We can visit Grandma though. She lives in the Strathcona Hotel in downtown Victoria. Would you like to visit her next weekend?"

"Yes."

The next weekend my mother, Elizabeth and I put on our best clothes and caught the Esquimalt streetcar. I didn't like the Strathcona Hotel. The narrow hallways smelled of cooked turnips and cigarette smoke. When we entered Grandma's room there was a pall of bluish-grey smoke hanging about a foot from the ceiling. My mother gave her a quick kiss on the cheek.

"Good Heavens, Mother! Do you have to smoke so much?"

Grandma rolled her eyes at my mother and lit a fresh cigarette. I could see that she didn't intend to be bossed around by my mother or by anyone else.

"Well, John, how do you like your new school?" Grandma asked me.

## Christmas in Victoria

I told Grandma that I liked Uppie's nature walks and that I was good at History. She smiled.

"I'm glad to hear that you're doing well. I've heard that Glenlyon is a very good school. Would you like a chocolate bar?"

My eyes lit up. A chocolate bar would be a real treat. Grandma went to her dresser, opened a drawer and pulled out two chocolate bars, one for Elizabeth and one for myself.

"You may have a piece now," my mother said, "and then you'll have to put the rest of it away for later."

When I opened my chocolate bar I noticed some white mouldy-looking stuff on it.

"I bought these chocolate bars for you quite a while ago. I was waiting for your mother to bring you for a visit. Never mind the white stuff. Just scrape it off when you get home. It'll be fine."

Then Grandma brought out some old photographs to share with my mother. She smoked the whole time. She had a way of exhaling slowly and then letting the smoke rise up through her nostrils. Every so often she blew a smoke ring. Maybe when I grew up I could learn to blow smoke rings. It looked like great fun, but each time she blew a ring my mother glared at her. When Grandma had finished with the photographs she brought out a yellowing pack of cards and taught me how to play rummy. Elizabeth was too young to

## Christmas in Victoria

learn cards, so she had to be content to play on the floor with a glass ornament – a pale green cat.

My mother grumbled all the way home on the streetcar.

"I wish she wouldn't smoke like that. It's disgusting the way she lets the smoke go back up her nose. I wouldn't mind if she'd just smoke properly like other people."

Maybe Grandma was the reason why my mother never smoked.

On Christmas Day Grandma was allowed into the Dockyard so she could have Christmas dinner with us. It was great fun having Grandma and the Beeches and our family all together. We had a large roast chicken with gravy and mashed potatoes, Brussel sprouts and yams. For dessert we had Jap oranges we could peel ourselves, Brazil nuts which we called "nigger-toes", Malaga raisins which had been dried right on their stems and marzipans. The very best thing was having crackers at the table. After we had eaten the main course we pulled the crackers and then opened them to find the "surprises". They all had paper hats, trinkets and jokes inside. Nobody even mentioned the war.

On Boxing Day we went by streetcar to the Uplands where my mother's Uncle Jim and Auntie Clara lived. They lived right at the end of the line where the Uplands streetcar made a loop before heading back to Victoria. They lived in a sprawling single-storey house with white painted stucco.

There was a gaudy gold wreath on the front door and lights strung through the trees. Everything about it looked like a photograph from a magazine.

"Humph!" said my mother. "Give me a good old two storey house any day. Real estate," my mother whispered to me. "Uncle Jim made all his money selling real estate."

She sniffed deprecatingly in the direction of the house. Uncle Jim must have been watching us through the frosted window at the side of his front door because he opened the door as soon as Uncle Roy rang the doorbell. He appeared at the door in a perfectly pressed pearl-grey woolen suit and a waistcoat with a golden watch-chain. He was smoking a long cigar and was sticking a toothpick between two gold teeth. He made an appreciative sucking noise as he removed whatever was stuck there.

"Wal, Merry Christmas everybody. Ethel, Bea, Roy, Winifred, and um, um…"

"John and Elizabeth."

"And um, um…."

"Marjorie, David and Joanne," Uncle Roy looked annoyed, and the tiny veins around his nose started to go red.

"Uh-huh," Uncle Jim grunted. He seemed to have lost interest at this point and was looking over our heads and out onto the road. Then he lowered his head and fixed my mother with a piercing gaze. "And how are you, Winifred?"

"I'm feeling fine." She gave Uncle Jim a sharp look. "But I'm getting cold."

There were obviously some bad feelings between Uncle Jim and my mother, but I had no idea what they were. Nobody ever spoke to me about such adult matters.

"Wal, don't just stand there. Come on in. Make yourself at home and get warm."

Once inside we were greeted by Auntie Clara. She was much younger than Uncle Jim. Her hair was perfectly coiffed and she wore bright rouge on both cheeks. She kissed Grandma on both cheeks, leaving rouge marks on each of them.

"Ethel, I'll swear you look younger every time I see you. Do make yourself comfortable. And Winifred and Bea and Roy. How good of you all to come. It wouldn't be Christmas without you. And…and"

"Marjorie, David and Joanne," Uncle Roy grumped.

"John and Elizabeth," my mother added coldly.

"Well, well, how you all have grown. Do have a sandwich."

Auntie Clara was traveling around the room with a large silver tray covered with tiny sandwiches with their crusts cut off. Inside them was some kind of pinkish-grey spread. I picked up two but when I realized that my mother was glaring at me I put one back. I looked around the living room. It was like no living room I had ever seen before. The chairs had bright pink and lime-green satin covers and skinny wooden legs. There was a love seat with alternating black, red and yellow stripes. If you looked quickly around the room you felt dizzy. There were large gilt-framed pictures of landscapes sprinkled liberally about the walls. Aunt Clara noticed that I was carefully surveying the art display. They looked nothing like the somber seascapes we had on our walls at Sunny Corner.

"Aren't they wonderful. Your Uncle Jim and I bought them in Paris just before the war. We bought them for a fraction of what they were worth."

As soon as Auntie Clara was out of ear-shot my mother nudged me in the direction of the furniture and whispered in my ear.

"Not real antiques!"

In one corner of the living room there was a highly-polished black grand piano. On one corner of the piano was a photograph of a handsome young man in an Air Force uniform.

"That's their son, Richard," my mother whispered. "He was in the RCAF. Shot down and killed in action."

I felt sorry for these poor people who had lost a son, but my mother might as well have saved her breath. Uncle Jim moved to the photograph and started speaking to all assembled in a loud voice.

"Shot down and killed over Europe where the real war is." Uncle Jim shot a glance at Uncle Roy who was standing there in his full naval uniform. Uncle Roy turned beet red but said nothing.

*"My goodness,"* I thought. *"That was really rude. Hasn't Uncle Jim heard about the Weser?"*

There were other guests. Uncle Jim's older brother, Uncle Geoffrey, was there with his wife Auntie Adelaide. He smoked a cigar that was even bigger than Uncle Jim's. When Elizabeth and I were introduced to him he only grunted. Auntie Adelaide smiled at us but she was so obese that her eye-lids and cheeks seemed to merge. Could she really see us?

"That's nice," she said, and moved off to speak to some other guests.

Uncle Philip and Auntie Doreen were nice, especially Auntie Doreen. She had a girl Elizabeth's age and spent a lot of time talking to Elizabeth about dolls and stuff like that. Then she spotted Joanne, chucked her under the chin and went "Goo goo goo." That was what you were supposed to say to babies when they were being held and were too young to talk back.

## Christmas in Victoria

Grandma was having a wonderful time. She smoked one cigarette after another and exhaled all the smoke right up through her nostrils. She walked around to everyone in the party and told them how nice they looked. Uncle Jim had to fill his silver cigarette box twice just to keep her satisfied. My mother was looking more and more irritated.

"For goodness sakes, Mother," my mother whispered to her as soon as she had an opportunity but Grandma just smiled and kept on smoking.

Then Uncle Clarence showed up at the door.

"Wal, Clarence," Uncle Jim said, "fancy seeing you here. So glad you were able to come. How on earth did you manage to make it all the way in from Sooke? How have you been keeping anyway?"

Uncle Jim looked embarrassed and kept up a stream of questions. Uncle Clarence stuttered a reply to each one. No, he wouldn't eat a meat sandwich, but a stick of celery would suit him just fine.

"Now how about a good stiff drink, Clarence?"

"No. No. J - just a little ice w - water, th - thank you."

"Cigarette?"

"No, th - thank you. I haven't taken up the habit."

By this time Uncle Clarence had attracted a few stares.

## Christmas in Victoria

"A little eccentric," my mother whispered in my ear. "I'll tell you later."

Then I met Uncle Osbert and Auntie Bella. Uncle Osbert had a kind word for everyone, but Auntie Bella never allowed him to finish a sentence. She continually interrupted him to make sure that he had all his facts straight.

"You understand of course," Auntie Bella said, "that Osbert has no idea of how to read a map. Do you Ozzie dear"

"We'd be sitting pretty today, but Osbert just had to buy shares in that copper mine. You were taken, weren't you Ozzie?"

I thought Uncle Osbert was the nicest person at the whole party, and I hated the way Auntie Bella kept interrupting and criticizing him for every little thing. By then I had eaten enough of the little sandwiches and was tired of the party. I wanted to go home. So apparently did my mother and Uncle Roy and Auntie Bea. They thanked Uncle Jim and Auntie Clara for a wonderful time and headed outside to wait for the Uplands streetcar.

Once they were on the streetcar my mother and Auntie Bea got the giggles, and that was when I got all the gossip. Auntie Clara was Spanish and twenty years younger than Uncle Jim. He married her because she was pretty and knew how to entertain guests. Uncle Jim had pots of money and terrible taste. He had paid a fortune for all that gaudy

## Christmas in Victoria

furniture in Paris, and if the truth be known no self-respecting furniture dealer in Victoria would think of selling such rubbish. Uncle Geoffrey was losing his memory, but it didn't really matter because he didn't care who anyone was anyway. Auntie Adelaide had diabetes from eating too many creampuffs and macaroons and was probably going blind. Uncle Osbert was hen-pecked publicly by Auntie Bella. He was a nice, gentle man but nobody had any respect for him. Auntie Bella was a fierce Presbyterian who believed in eating porridge and always having her facts straight. Uncle Philip and Auntie Doreen were nice kind steady people and so there was really nothing else to be said about them.

I looked at Grandma carefully. Didn't she mind hearing her brothers criticized like this? She didn't seem to care and just kept fishing in her purse for cigarettes so she could light up as soon as she got off the streetcar.

So that was how I spent my first Christmas in Victoria. Christmas was for children and Uncle Jim. New Years was just for grown-ups to have cocktail parties and after that it was back to school.

# CHAPTER 9

# LESSONS ON THE FARM

Shortly after Christmas I received a letter from Reading. It had David Walker's address on it, but it didn't look like his handwriting. I opened hoping to find a belated Christmas card. No such good fortune. It was a note from his mother telling me in a kind way that David had passed away, the victim of a heart aneurism. I showed it to my mother who nodded. She must have already heard the news. I was filled with sadness. When and if I ever returned to England there would be no David Walker there for me to visit. No stamp trading, no model trains and no Canon Rowe.

I just had to accept it and settle into a routine at school. I did well in most of my classes, played soccer at Windsor Park in the cold and the damp, caught the streetcar twice a day, walked home past the grim brick buildings in the Dockyard, did my homework, played with my lead soldiers in front of the fireplace and listened to the BBC News.

The news was not good. The Germans had conquered Yugoslavia and Greece. That meant that they had now conquered the whole of South-eastern Europe. Then Hitler sent Rommel and the Afrika Corps to North Africa where they pushed the British troops back towards Cairo. The Suez Canal was under threat.

In June two extraordinary things happened. The Germans invaded Russia and I came first in my form at school. Some people thought the German invasion of Russia might prove their undoing. After all, hadn't Napoleon made the same error?

When I came first in my form it meant two things. It meant that I had won a book prize. The book was "A Child's History of the World" by V.M Hillyer. I treasured it. It also meant that I was allowed to skip a form. I felt proud that I had done so well but I was a little fearful at the same time. I was already in the smallest boy in the school, and now I would be placed in a form with boys who were even bigger. What if I couldn't keep up with them when we played games? What if they bullied me?

Simmie believed that, if he thought the boys were capable of doing work in a higher form, they should be allowed the opportunity. I wanted desperately to live up to his expectations so I readily agreed to skip the Second Form.

I didn't really have time to think about what it would be like for me, because then something even more wonderful happened. My mother took Grandma and Elizabeth and me to Rawdie's and Nita's farm for the holidays. Their farm was

Lessons on the Farm

in Metchosin. It wasn't like a real farm with cows and horses and rows of vegetables. It was actually a chicken ranch with several chicken houses. Some of them were near the farmhouse where Rawdie and Nita lived. Some of them were right at the edge of the forest. Rawdie and Nita were my second cousins, something like uncle and aunt but not as close. We didn't stay in the big farm-house with them. Instead we stayed in a small white house we called "The Cottage". There were hollyhocks growing in front and a lilac bush to the side. It looked like a storybook cottage.

*11: At the Cottage*

## Lessons on the Farm

When I stepped outside of the cottage I could see right across the Strait of Juan de Fuca to the Olympic Mountains. The sun shone, the water in the strait sparkled and I was happy. There was a whole hillside filled with broom. Rawdie loaned me a hatchet and I cut trails through the broom. I could tiptoe through a trail, sneak up on a Nazi sentry, cut his throat with my hatchet and disappear down another trail where the German soldiers would never find me.

When I walked up the road into the farm I had to pass over a metal grating called a cow-catcher. I had to be careful. If my foot fell into the cow-catcher sideways I could twist my ankle or even break it.

Just past the cow-catcher was a cottage that seemed not much bigger than a playhouse. This was where Gee lived. Gee was a Chinaman. He lived all by himself in the tiny cottage and tended a small garden where he grew all his own vegetables. He wore ragged work clothes and a straw hat called a *coolie* hat to keep the sun off his head. He smiled as soon as he saw me and invited me to help him collect eggs with him every morning. That became my job. Gee carried a bucket and I went ahead and reached underneath the chickens and pulled out the warm eggs; white eggs from the white chickens and brown eggs from the brown chickens. Sometimes the chickens protested but they never tried to hurt me. Once they got used to seeing me they would let me pet them. Even though they lived in dusty pens their feathers were always white and shiny. Sometimes the roosters tried to frighten me away but they got used to me too, and after a while they didn't pay any attention.

Gee hardly knew any English so he didn't talk to me much, but he always had a friendly smile. Rawdie and Nita explained to me that he sent his wages to his family in China to keep them from starving, but always put aside just enough so that he could have his bones shipped home to China when he died. I thought that must be a terribly lonely life with no wife and children to keep him company. I wondered if he worried about his family. I had been told that there was a Japanese army in China murdering people and doing other terrible things. Was his family safe?

After supper I played cards with Grandma. We played either *Snap* or *Rummy*. I always beat her at Snap because I was faster and practically always beat her at Rummy because I was better at remembering which cards were in the discard pile. She was good-natured and never minded when I beat her. Occasionally we played *Cheat*. We were allowed to yell "Snap!" even if the discarded cards weren't identical. If we thought the other person was cheating we could yell out "Cheat!" My grandmother always got confused and wound up hating the game. I felt sorry for her after a while and didn't ask to play Cheat any more.

When I was tired of cards there were books to read. My favourite book was the one I had just won at Glenlyon. It told me all sorts of interesting things like how the Earth began as gas shooting into space from the sun and how it slowly cooled off enough for the oceans to form and for life to begin. The other book I enjoyed was one I found on a shelf in the cabin. It was called "American Natural History". It was filled with drawings of grizzly bears, ferocious jaguars, strange sloths, huge anacondas which lived in the Amazon River and grew to over 30 feet and a great variety of poisonous snakes.

Snakes fascinated me. There were snakes, hundreds of them living in the tall grass between our cottage and the farmhouse. They were only garter snakes but I could pretend they were dangerous South American snakes. I had my B.B. gun with me at the farm and proceeded to hunt them down. To show what a great hunter I was I began tacking their bodies to the outside of our cottage. Their bodies kept moving up and down even after they were dead. Grandma was horrified and too frightened to go outside.

I wanted my mother to tell me to end this disgusting game and tell me to take the snakes down, but she didn't. Perhaps she enjoyed Grandma's discomfort. After a while I took the snakes down without being asked. Then I felt more at peace with myself.

The pathways through the broom were thick with grasshoppers. One day I stole a box of kitchen matches from the kitchen and began catching grasshoppers. When I was sure I was alone I stuffed several grasshoppers into the box and set it on fire. After the box had burned up I was able to see what the grasshoppers looked like when they were dead. The ones on the outer side of the box were charred but the ones on the inside looked as though they had been toasted. Then I worried about whether they had suffered or whether they had died instantly. If they had suffered I would have been no better than a Nazi. I resolved never to cremate innocent insects again. A few days later it occurred to me that I could have set the whole hillside on fire by playing with matches. I felt ashamed for having put the whole beautiful countryside at risk.

Once a week my mother walked Elizabeth and me to the Metchosin General Store. My mother gave me an allowance of ten cents a week and I was allowed to spend it on chewing gum, something that would never be allowed at either the Dockyard or at school. One penny was enough to buy a tiny packet containing two "Chiclets". I had a choice of flavours – Doublemint, Spearmint, Pepsin, Retsin and Cinnamon. After my purchase I had nine cents left over that I could save.

"I don't mind you chewing gum out here in the country, but keep your mouth closed," my mother told me. "I don't want to see the inside of your mouth."

*"Fair enough,"* I thought. I felt a surge of freedom standing outside the store, basking in the sun and chewing a chiclet. I was wearing a white open-necked short-sleeve shirt and

khaki shorts. Such a relief after the scratchy grey shirt and grey flannel shorts I had to wear every day to school.

Metchosin had some names I found amusing. Kangaroo Road. Were there actually kangaroos hiding in the woods? Not likely but how did it get its name? Whiffen Spit. Did people smell something rotten there and then have to spit? Then on the road to Victoria there was Witty's Lagoon. Did funny things happen there? Everything about Metchosin sparked my imagination.

Perhaps there were some other amusing places I could explore. One day I walked to the chicken house that was farthest from the farmhouse and then walked behind it. There was a trail that led into the forest. Here was a place I could begin my exploration. It wasn't long before the trail stopped being a trail. I had imagined that if I kept walking I would come to a sunny clearing or a grassy meadow. Or a grove of arbutus trees with shiny orange bark glistening in the afternoon sun. Or perhaps a tiny pebbly beach that no-one else knew about. No such luck. Just plain old fir trees and plenty of them.

Perhaps I should turn back. No, that would be boring. Perhaps if I simply continued through the forest I would find the magical place I was seeking. So I plunged onward into the forest. There was no magical place. The trees were blocking the sun now and the forest looked the same in every direction. I thought of Snow White lost in the forest

## Lessons on the Farm

with the trees grabbing at her. I suddenly felt cold as I summed up my situation. The truth was that I was lost, perhaps hopelessly lost.

What should I do? My first reaction was to run as fast as I could and then perhaps I would eventually burst out of the forest. Breathless and fearful I began to run. Luck was with me. I did come out onto a road, a winding dirt road. Perhaps if I waited long enough someone would come along and rescue me. And that was exactly what happened. A dusty Model T Ford came around the bend and squealed to a halt in a swirl of dust. There were two very dark men in it, one driving and the other in the passenger seat. I swallowed my fear and told them I was lost.

"Where you want go?"

"The Matthews Chicken Farm."

The two men grunted and motioned me into the back seat.

"You put feet up. Plenty fish on floor."

And there I sat with my feet resting on sacks full of smelly fish. But I was still worried. Who were these strange dark men who said practically nothing? Perhaps they meant to kidnap me and hold me for ransom.

But nothing bad happened. They knew where Rawdie's farm was and dropped me at the foot of the road leading up to the farm.

"Thank you."

"Uuhh-huh."

What a relief when our whitewashed summer cottage finally came into view. I was back at The Farm and safe! I thought my mother would look relieved but she didn't. She looked annoyed, and then I had to explain how I had found my way back to The Farm. When I had finished telling her about the men in the Model T she looked even more annoyed.

"I'm very cross," she said. "Those were Indians! And you actually got into the back of their filthy car with all that fish." She wrinkled her nose in disgust. "You'd better have a bath before you go to bed tonight."

"But I've already had a bath this week."

We were only supposed to have a bath once a week with four inches of water in it. That was how often King George and Queen Elizabeth bathed and that was how much water they used. It was because of the war and they were setting an example for us. We weren't supposed to waste fuel or take too much interest in our personal appearance.

"I don't care. I'm making an exception this week. I'm not having you sitting around our cottage reeking of fish."

I groaned inwardly. Having a bath was a laborious process with my mother heating up kettles full of water on the wood stove and pouring them into an enamel tub with me getting little or no privacy. I sniffed my clothes. There was nothing wrong with them. The smell must have been in my mother's imagination.

I learned a lot about different races of people that summer. I learned that Chinamen lived alone, worked hard. and sent money to China. I learned that Indians did almost no work at all and drove around in old cars with fish in the back seat where the passengers were supposed to go. I already knew that Germans were sadistic and stupid, so I was adding to my knowledge all the time. I could also tell that my mother held the Chinese in high esteem because they worked so hard.

One day a robin with a wounded wing scampered under the lilac bush. I tried to coax it out but it kept running around in circles.

"Mummy, there's a wounded robin under the lilac bush. What should I do?"

"Just shoot it. Now don't bother me. I'm busy darning your socks."

I was shocked. I had wanted my mother to help me catch it and make a little nest with cotton wool where it could recover while I fed it worms.

The temptation to use my B.B. gun got the better of me. One shot and the robin was lying lifeless under the lilac bush with a blue veil over its eyes. Once again I had become the same evil boy who shot snakes and roasted grasshoppers. Why couldn't I have simply disobeyed my mother and helped the robin or at least have just left it alone? I fished out the body from under the bush and dug a shallow grave for it. Then I found a couple of twigs and tied them together with some of my mother's darning wool to make a cross for the grave.

That night my mother appeared in my dreams as a witch. Surely there must be something wrong with her. She was impatient with my grandmother and had no feelings for wounded birds. But what was I to do? She was the only mother I had. Maybe in the future she would change and begin to behave more in the way I thought a mother should.

CHAPTER 10

# The World is Coming Apart

I hated it when I had to go back to the Dockyard and school at the beginning of September. I thought that if I could just stay at the farm it would be summer forever. Instead I was sentenced once more to the grey grim Dockyard with all its reminders of war and my grey school uniform. But there was always next summer. I could come to the farm again. At least I thought I could.

On the first day of school I looked around the classroom to see who my new classmates were. Jim and Bob Webster were twins. The story was that Jim had been born a few minutes ahead of Bob, and that was why he was bigger and smarter than Bob. He was bigger and he certainly acted as though he were smarter and more important. The masters always called us by our surnames and never by our first names so the Webster twins were addressed as Webster One and Webster Two. Perhaps being called Webster One was part of the reason why Jim felt that he was smarter than Bob.

## The World is Coming Apart

Then the masters decided that they should tease him and ask him difficult questions so that he didn't get a swelled head.

"So ye think ye're smart do ye, Webster One? Perhaps ye can tell me the name of Tennyson's longest poem. Ye don't know, do ye? Now find out by Monday morning and report back to me. No, don't smile at me, ye rubbishy fellow. I'm not going to forget over the weekend and if ye don't know I'll put ye in my pocket."

Bob Webster was quiet and wore glasses. I liked him because he gave thoughtful answers in class instead of cheeky ones like his older brother. He would have made a nice friend if I had been a year or two older.

Jim Webster was not the only boy who was full of himself. Sean Montmorency was full of himself too, but in a different way. He had an uncle who was a British general, and liked to draw attention to himself by telling jokes that weren't really funny. The other boys groaned when he started to tell a joke because they knew in advance that there was going to be something amiss by the time he reached the punch line.

Bradley Vowell the Second looked important. He was the son of Bradley Vowell the First who was important because he was the president of a large bank in the United States. Bradley wore a vest under his grey jacket, and every so often he would pull out a large watch from his vest pocket so that he could see what time it was. The fact that his head was very large in relation to the rest of his body made the rest of us think that he probably had a large brain. When he went out for recess he never played games with the other boys. He just stood there observing everyone and looking at his watch.

As far as the other boys were concerned Jim Webster was a natural leader. We automatically listened to him and followed his instructions, Sean Montmorency was irritating because of his flat jokes, Bradley Vowell the Second was simply ignored. Simmie must have noticed that the other boys paid attention to Jim Webster because he made Jim a prefect. That meant that he was expected to help organize play equipment at recess and boss the other boys if necessary. But he was only allowed to boss us with small things, not with big things like the masters did. On Monday morning we waited in vain to find out if Jim had found out the name of Tennyson's longest poem. I suspected that if Jim was to become a prefect, then Simmie wouldn't want to embarrass him. He would want us to respect him.

I had several other new classmates. Philip Hoskins was overweight, and was poor at sports. We suspected that his mother had managed to sneak an extra ration book just for him. We thought that all fat people were happy and that made it all right for us to tease him.

Roger Geoffrey had eczema but no-one would have thought of teasing him. It didn't seem right to tease someone with a skin condition he couldn't help. He commanded a lot of

## The World is Coming Apart

respect because he was good at sports and always played fair. His father, like Uncle Roy, was a naval officer.

We didn't tease Clarence Mason either. Clarence had skinny arms that didn't work very well because he had suffered from polio when he was younger. He was excused from gym classes but we didn't make fun of him because having had polio wasn't his fault. Clarence was an American but he was living in Victoria because his father was a consul or something like that.

Bill Carrington had perpetually rosy cheeks and always seemed slightly out of breath. That was because he was always on some kind of mission such as retrieving a soccer ball that had been caught by the wind and sent sailing down onto the beach. The masters were always giving him jobs like cleaning the blackboard erasers or collecting the wickets after a game of cricket. Nobody thought of accusing him of being a teacher's pet though. He was just as nice to his fellow pupils and would be the first to help you extract gravel from your knee if you fell off your bicycle. He was a nice person so it would have been wrong to tease him.

Bill's English cousin, Rod Peary, was a different kind of person altogether. Just as Bill took everything seriously, Rod took almost nothing seriously. He was the class clown. One day Uppie pointed to the world map and asked Rod if he could locate Peru.

"I think it's right underneath the Neilson's chocolate bar, sir. Is that a trick question?"

Uppie went into a rage and attacked Rod with a yardstick. Rod hid under his desk and Uppie demolished the yardstick by slashing it against the desk. without ever managing to touch Rod in the process. We didn't dare laugh because the whole episode had put Uppie into a foul mood, and we didn't want him to cancel our Nature Study walks.

Nobody could quite figure Rod out. He was either very stupid or very smart. Either way we all liked him because he kept us entertained when our classes became boring.

My friend Richard Preston was also allowed to skip Form II and go into Form III with me. I was really glad to have him as a friend because he was my own age. It felt good to have someone I considered my equal in my new class, especially someone as good-natured as he was.

When Uppie taught us boxing, he always matched me up with Richard because we were the same age. Richard always got the better of me in boxing and every time he hit me in the nose it started to bleed. But Richard was kind. Whenever he saw my nose starting to bleed he stopped the match. My mother got fed up with me coming home with blood on my shirts, so she took me to a doctor in Victoria to have the blood vessels in my nose cauterized. That turned out to be a good idea because I didn't get nosebleeds after that.

## The World is Coming Apart

One thing about being with the older boys that I didn't like was having to do *cross country* runs as part of our Gym program. We had to run all the way from the school to Cattle Point in the Uplands and then back again. Uppie had a clipboard and a stopwatch and he marked down exactly how long it took us. I always had a stitch in my side by the time I reached Cattle Point. The stitch was caused by running too far and too fast for my size, but I didn't dare walk instead. The other boys would have thought I was a sissy and Uppie would have believed I was just being lazy. I usually came in last or just ahead of Philip Hoskins and Bradley Vowell the Second. This was little consolation because Philip was obviously too fat to run properly and Bradley didn't care one way or the other.

Now that Russia was in the war going back and forth from the Dockyard to school had become more interesting. There were now pictures of Russian warplanes printed on the Sweet Caporal packets and I wanted to collect all of them as fast as I could. Snappy-looking fighter planes called Yaks and Migs.

One day I was so intent on looking for packets when I got off the Oak Bay streetcar downtown that I missed the Esquimalt streetcar. By the time the next streetcar arrived I had to pee. Then by the time the streetcar was half way home I was in agony. I retreated to the back of the streetcar and when I thought that no-one was looking I peed on the floor. Shortly after I had finished the streetcar began its descent down Signal Hill. The floor of the streetcar consisted of grooved wooden boards which made a perfect river course. Before long my pool of pee had flowed down to the front of the streetcar and right beside the conductor. He either didn't notice or pretended not to notice. When the streetcar stopped outside the Dockyard I ran home as fast as I could leaving the conductor to deal with the mess I'd made. After that embarrassing episode I made sure never to get onto a streetcar with a full bladder.

Despite the addition of the fine-looking Russian fighter planes the war continued to go badly. In the Fall of 1941 Rommel's Afrika Corps was poised to take the Suez Canal, the Germans had advanced deep into Russia, and German U-boats were sinking Allied ships in the Atlantic at a record rate. I was still asked to take on the role of Hitler when we played war games at recess, but there was much less enthusiasm for these games than in the previous year. Perhaps it was because the war was dragging on and there were so few Allied victories to raise our spirits.

Glenlyon School was situated above the beach. If you looked across the water from the school you could see Discovery Island and Chatham Island. And then if you looked farther still and it was a clear day you could see San Juan Island on the American side of the border. And then if you looked to the south you could see the waters of Juan de Fuca Strait. One day I saw two large warships traveling through the

## The World is Coming Apart

strait faster than I believed any ship could possibly travel. Where could they possibly be going?

I mentioned my sighting at the dinner table that night but everyone else simply looked blank. You weren't supposed to talk about ship movements. In fact Victoria and Esquimalt were full of posters that said things like "Loose Lips Sink Ships". One of the posters had a picture of a sailor drinking beer with a sneaky looking woman in a slinky blouse. There was a small inset picture of Hitler in the corner so you knew right away that the woman was a spy.

After dinner one of the stewards took me aside.

"What you saw were the battleships H.M.S. *Prince of Wales* and H.M.S. *Repulse*. They refueled here last night on their way to Singapore. Don't you dare tell anyone I told you or I'd be court-martialed and I don't know what would happen to you. You'd probably be expelled from that fancy school you go to every day."

I never said another word to anyone about the ships, but I couldn't help wondering. Why were they going to Singapore when the war was being fought in Europe?

I didn't have to wait long for an answer. On December 7, Japanese bombers launched a surprise attack on Pearl Harbour in Hawaii and sank most of the American fleet while it was sitting at anchor. It seemed unbelievable that they could sink a whole navy in a single raid.

## The World is Coming Apart

Right after Pearl Harbour the *Prince Robert* left the Dockyard with Canadian troops who were supposed to protect Hong Kong from the Japanese.

On December 10, Japanese dive bombers sank both the *Repulse* and the *Prince of Wales* off the coast of Malaya. So that was the answer to my question about why these warships were heading for Singapore. The British must have known in advance that war with Japan was a likelihood. They must have thought that the *Repulse* and *Prince of Wales* would be enough to frighten the Japanese away from Malaya. Both ships were sunk by Japanese dive bombers because neither of them had any air cover.

The Japanese moved quickly through South-East Asia. They invaded the Philippines and Malaya. On Christmas Day they captured Hong Kong. The Canadian soldiers who had gone to protect the British colony were now either dead or taken captive. There were terrible tales of wounded soldiers being hauled out of their hospital beds and being used for bayonet practice and of the nurses being raped by Japanese soldiers. I didn't know what *raped* meant but I knew that it was something really bad that the Japs did to defenceless women.

Right after Pearl Harbour the Admirals House was shrouded in blackout curtains. We understood that if Pearl Harbour was a target the Dockyard in Esquimalt might be the next target. The Japanese were roaming the Pacific Ocean with their aircraft carriers and dive bombers and could show up here at any time. There was a lot of talk at dinnertime about the Japanese fishing boats on the West Coast. They might radio information to the Japanese Navy and tell them where our ships were located.

I was afraid. It was very different from being in England with the Germans on the other side of the English Channel sending over bombers every day. Then if they landed we could fight them on our school grounds with pitchforks we had borrowed from farmers. But what could we do about an enemy that might be anywhere in vast Pacific Ocean? What if they landed here screaming "Banzai Nippon!" and using us for bayonet practice?

I was ten years old and by now I had a firm idea about what was happening in the world. There was a gigantic struggle underway between good and evil. We were good. The Nazis and Japs were evil. If they won the war the Japanese would have the West Coast and we would all be subjected to unimaginable tortures. The Germans would control the rest of North America and turn everyone into robots shouting *Heil Hitler!* The world as we knew it would be totally destroyed.

I returned to school in January of 1942 in a gloomy mood. There was little evidence of success in the war against the Nazis and now the Japanese were almost at our doorstep. Fortunately the playground offered us an opportunity to vanquish our new foe. Casting began immediately. I had successfully played Hitler in 1941. Was it too much to hope for that I could play the lead role in the war against Japan?

We looked each other over carefully. I was small, I had buckteeth, black hair, heavy eye-lids, and a tendency to blink and squint even though my eye-sight was perfect. Once again I became an overnight star.

"Okay, Hemy, you can be Hirohito."

"And Tojo too if you want."

I stuck out my teeth, narrowed my eyes and grabbed a nearby stick for my samurai sword.

"Aaah So! Are you ready to die for your emperor?"

"Banzai Nippon!" came the reply and the game was on. Bill Carrington oozed goodness and bravery so he was chosen to play Johnny Canuck, Guardian of the North and hero of Dime Comics. One of the comic book scenarios had Canadian prisoners of the Japanese tied by their wrists to a kind of a maypole. The idea was that, as the prisoners spun faster and faster, they would fly into space one by one to be impaled on the bayonets of their Japanese captors. Fiendish! Sadistic monsters! At the last moment Johnny Canuck appeared on the scene and began knocking the Japanese soldiers about like bowling pins. Pow! Zap! Once the hapless Japs were lying in a heap Johnny Canuck was able to free the

Canadian prisoners. He was a truly Canadian hero and needed no help from the American Superman.

I never got to play Johnny Canuck but my obsession with the evil Japanese proved to be my undoing. When we came to school in the morning we were expected to be clean, have polished black shoes, a properly knotted tie and our hair carefully brushed into place. In order to ensure that our hair was in place we could choose, with parental guidance of course, between two products. One was *Brylcreem*, which came in a tube. *Brylcreem* felt nice and cool and didn't leave your hands greasy. *Brilliantine* on the other hand came in an oval can and did leave your hands greasy. You used *Brilliantine* if you wanted your hair to be flat and shiny like Edward VIII's. I liked *Brylcreem* but detested *Brilliantine*.

One of my classmates preferred Brilliantine. One day at recess in the middle of a war game I shouted out an insult.

"You have Japanese shit in your hair!"

Did that come out of me? I was in shock. Never in my life before had I used such foul language. My classmates looked appalled. And then they began backing away from me until I was standing alone on the playground. But my classmates weren't looking at me. They were looking above me and into the window of the masters' common room. The common room was where the masters congregated to smoke at recess. Its position facing the playground gave the masters an excellent opportunity to view their pupils at play.

I turned around and looked up at the common room window. Just as I feared. The masters were all standing and staring at me. They must have heard my outburst of vile language. I fully expected Simmie to come roaring out of the common room and drag me off to the sunroom for a caning. But he didn't. Nothing happened. I slunk away from the vicinity of the common room and waited. I expected that one of the masters would have something serious to say to me when classes resumed. But nothing happened there either.

It was Friday and I went home for the weekend without having once been confronted. I concluded that what I had said and done was so serious that the masters would have to confer over the weekend about how they should deal with me. Perhaps Simmie intended to give me a good thrashing with his cane and then expel me from the school. That would mean that I would either have to go to a public school where I would be beaten up by ruffians every day or sent to a different private school where the headmaster was reputed to use a bullwhip rather than a cane.

The other thing that I had to contemplate over the weekend was that I had undoubtedly committed a mortal sin by using that kind of language. It was probably all right for Protestants to be foul-mouthed because they didn't know any better and were going to go to Hell anyway but it was totally unacceptable for a Catholic like myself. What if I were run over by a streetcar in the next 48 hours? I might go straight to Hell, or at least to Purgatory where I would have hundreds or thousands of years to contemplate my misdeed.

Should I go to Confession? No. Kneeling in a confessional with a foul-breathed Irish priest on the other side of the screen was unthinkable.

By the time Monday morning rolled around I was a nervous wreck. I took the streetcar to school, stood by myself in a remote corner of the playground and waited for classes to begin. 9 a.m. Now I would learn my fate.

Nothing happened. The masters treated me as though nothing had happened. The other boys seemed to have forgotten that I was a menace, and wanted me to resume my role as Emperor Hirohito. It then occurred to me that, because nothing had happened to me, it was just possible that my crime was not as large as I had first imagined.

But I played it safe, and never used bad language on the playground again. Not only that I learned to be more tolerant of the boys who used *Brilliantine*.

# CHAPTER 11

# BEING IN THE MOVIES

In the Winter of 1942 our fear of an attack by the Japanese continued as each day brought news of new Japanese successes in the Pacific. David and I shared the same bedroom. If the Japanese Navy were to attack we would be right on the front line as our bedroom faced directly onto to Strait of Juan de Fuca.

One morning David and I were getting dressed for breakfast and school when it seemed as though our worst fears were about to be realized. A huge shape loomed out of the fog. It was a ship, the largest ship I had ever seen, and it was heading straight toward us.

Surely this was it. It looked as though the ship were heading straight for the shoreline in front of the Admirals House. Perhaps it would crash into the shore and hundreds of screaming Japanese commandos would jump ashore and bayonet us. We held our breath. Then, just as it seemed as though the ship would hit the rocks, it made a sudden left angle turn. As it did we got a better view. It wasn't a Japanese aircraft carrier as we had feared. It wasn't even a warship. It looked like one of the CPR boats that travelled between Victoria and Vancouver, only several times larger. Then it disappeared into the fog again.

David and I came down to breakfast shaking with excitement.

"There was a huge ship. It was coming right towards us. It was as high as a skyscraper. We thought it was going to crash into us."

The adults at the breakfast table simply raised their eyebrows, and urged us not to talk about it at school. It would be better if we were to say nothing. It was wartime and we weren't supposed to discuss ship movements. I wanted to be a war hero and what better way than to announce the arrival of a strange ship. It was frustrating to be told to shut up.

After a couple of days the secret was out. The ship was the *Queen Elizabeth,* the largest ship in the world and it had sailed into the Dockyard for a refit. With only inches to spare it had been coaxed into a drydock where an army of welders and riveters converted it into a troop ship. Hundreds of metal plates were welded onto the windows to prevent light from escaping from the cabins. If there had been a miscalculation and the huge ship had been unable to fit into the drydock it would have been a disaster. The Dockyard in Esquimalt had the only drydock on the West Coast large enough to accommodate the *Queen Elizabeth.*

Being in the Movies

I was aching to go down to the drydock to see this amazing ship, but I didn't stand a chance. The drydocks were *out of bounds* and that was that. For official purposes the *Queen Elizabeth* wasn't there at all. When the refit had been completed the ship left the Dockyard under cover of darkness, and we had no opportunity to see it again. We were not even allowed to say that it had left because it hadn't really been there in the first place.

Apart from the shared excitement, sharing a room with David was starting to get on my nerves. He was three years my senior and had interests that were quite different from mine. For one he had begun smuggling Esquire magazines into the bedroom. Esquire was considered a *naughty* magazine because it contained full page coloured drawings of *pin-ups girls*. David wanted me to look at them.

"Look at this one. She's Betty Grable. She's the sexiest pin-up of them all."

He showed me a picture of a woman with very long legs, large breasts and a sailor suit. An artist named Vargas had painted the picture for Esquire Magazine. I wasn't interested. If David was able to smuggle magazines into our room, why couldn't he have found one with pictures of warplanes and tanks? That would have been a lot more interesting.

My lack of interest didn't deter David in the slightest. More Esquire Magazines appeared with pictures of Rita

Hayworth and Veronica Lake, some by Vargas and some by another artist named Petty.

Veronica Lake had hair that hung down over the side of her head so that she could only see out of one eye.

"I think Veronica Lake is a drip," I said.

"Who's a drip, Drip?" he replied. That shut me up and I didn't offer any more criticisms.

Then David started smuggling in a magazine called Vogue. It was a fashion magazine of all things. Not only that, but David was actually copying the pictures into a scrapbook. His drawings were really good, but I couldn't for the life of me understand why he would be interested in fashions. Then he began designing and drawing fashions that were coming out of his imagination. I was jealous. David could draw a fashion model with just a few strokes of his pencil. When I drew planes or tanks or ships it took me much longer and the drawings never looked as good as David's. He obviously had some kind of talent that I lacked.

Next, David began copying the pin-ups from Esquire and designing clothes for them. From there he progressed to drawing his own pin-ups. Not only that, he was drawing them naked. I was shocked.

One evening at bedtime David was lying on top of his bed admiring one of the naked women he had drawn. Then he pulled off his pajama bottoms and started playing with his penis and laughing. I was really embarrassed. I pulled my bedcovers over my head and pretended to be asleep. What was David doing anyway? This was almost as bad as having to share my bedroom with the Delaney brothers when they were sniffing the ends of one another's fingers. I wanted a bedroom of my own so badly.

*"Please,"* I thought to myself, *"I want someone to make David stop this crazy behaviour."*

Then, almost as though he had been reading my thoughts, Uncle Roy appeared at the door. Uncle Roy had very fair skin and when he was angry he was quite terrifying. His face was red and the veins in his neck were sticking out. He was breathing heavily and his eyes looked crazy.

"Give me those drawings!" he shouted at David.

Before David could hand them over Uncle Roy had grabbed them and was starting to rip them up.

"Now you come here!" He lunged at David. David escaped to the bathroom. I could hear him locking the door behind him.

"You come out of there, David."

No answer.

Uncle Roy lunged at the door. He crashed up against the door several times before the door splintered and he was able to force his way in. I was in shock. I could hear David screaming for help. I didn't know exactly what was happening in the bathroom but it was like a nightmare with Uncle Roy yelling and pounding and David wailing. I jumped into bed, put my head under the covers and closed my eyes. When everything had quietened down I really did fall asleep.

When I came home from school the following day I ran upstairs to look at the bathroom door. To my great surprise the door had been replaced. I supposed that if you were the Commodore of the Pacific Fleet you could get a door replaced pretty quickly.

When I went downstairs for dinner there was no sign of David. He had been sent to a small spare bedroom without any dinner.

After that episode there were no more Esquire or Vogue magazines in evidence. No pinup drawings either. Peace had returned to our bedroom. I felt sorry for David because Uncle Roy had gone berserk and given him a terrible beating. But I also felt satisfaction from knowing that David had been put in his place for disturbing my peace of mind.

David was subdued after his ordeal and remained so for several weeks. He stopped going on about movie stars and pinups. That suited me perfectly because I didn't want to hear about them. Then one day just before the summer holidays he came bounding into our shared bedroom laughing and clapping his hands. Obviously something was up.

"Hey, wake up, Hemy!"

"I am awake."

"Guess what. I'm going to be in the movies!"

I didn't believe him. It was obvious that David's fascination with movie stars had affected his mind. Movies were made in Hollywood, not in Victoria.

"I don't believe you."

"Well, it's true. They're going to make a movie about a British Commando raid on Norway, and I get to be a Norwegian. The movie's going to be called "The Commandos Strike at Dawn"."

There had been stories on the BBC News about British Commando raids on the coast of Europe, so that part of it was possible. But a movie made here in Victoria? Not possible.

"That can't be true, David. Movies are made in Hollywood. You told me that yourself."

"They're making it here because it looks like Norway here. We have mountains and trees and snow and stuff. Just like they do in Norway. Do you suppose they could make a movie about Norway in Hollywood where it's all palm trees and beaches and bathing beauties? They couldn't possibly. What a stupid idea! No, they have to make the movie here. And I'm going to be in it."

The story unfolded. Uncle Roy was going to loan the *Prince David* to Hollywood. The *Prince David* was a CNR coastal ferry that had been converted into a warship. Armed with guns it looked pretty much like a real destroyer. That was what we had in Esquimalt to protect us if the Japanese Navy decided to attack. And now Uncle Roy was going to loan it to Hollywood for a movie. It didn't seem right.

"Why is your Dad doing this? Shouldn't the *Prince David* be right here protecting us?"

"It's not going that far. It's just going to Bamberton on the Malahat. You know, close to Goldstream where we have picnics some time."

"But there's a war on. Why are they using a naval ship to make a movie right in the middle of the war?"

"It'll help us win the war, stupid. It's for morale. You know, if we feel good we'll fight harder and win the war faster."

Gradually the explanation unfolded. Canada and the U.S. were sending ship convoys to Russia with war materials to help the Russians fight the German armies. But to get the supplies to the Russians the convoys had to pass around the northern part of Norway and from there to the Russian port of Murmansk. The Germans had been building air bases in

Being in the Movies

Norway and sending out fighter-bombers to attack the convoys. The Allied ship losses had been tremendous. The movie was to show the Commandos going ashore in Norway and destroying one of the German air bases. It didn't matter whether it was a true story or not. The movie would make it look like a true story and we would feel good about it. So many bad things had happened in the course of the war that we needed something to feel good about. So it all made sense.

"The Commandos go ashore at night," David explained. "They kill all the Germans in their beds and blow up their planes. Then they make their escape to England. Those lousy Krauts won't even know what hit them."

David explained it in a way that made it all seem reasonable. And exciting. And then a poisonous thought entered my mind.

"So how do *you* get to be in the movie?"

"Dad asked me. It's because I'm blond and look like a Norwegian. Marjorie's going to be in it too because she's blond."

"Do you think I could get a part in the movie?"

"Probably not. You don't look like a Norwegian to me. Your hair's almost black and you get a tan every time the sun comes out. You might get a part if they make a movie with Japs in it. You get to play Hirohito at school, don't you?"

Being in the Movies

I burned. That poisonous feeling that was creeping into my mind was jealousy. David was getting a break because he was blonde. And I didn't stand a chance because of my hair and complexion. How unfair! And another thing - David was supposed to be in the doghouse because of his drawings of nude women, and here was his dad being nice to him. But I couldn't admit to anyone including myself that I was jealous. I had learned at Glenlyon and before that at Reading Grammar School that I was supposed to hide my feelings, especially the bad ones like jealousy. It was called "keeping a stiff upper lip". It was something to do with "character". If you wanted to show that you had character you kept a stiff upper lip. In order to accomplish this I had to pretend not to care.

When Summer holidays began a blue Canadian Navy bus came to pick up Marjorie and David to go to Bamberton I could hardly stand it. More than anything else I wanted a part in that movie. The worst part was when David and Marjorie returned from the movie set in the evening. Each of them had been paid a whole dollar that they could spend on chewing gum or anything else they wanted.

"Hey!" David shouted, "Making movies is fun. And we get paid for having fun."

A whole dollar just for being in a stupid movie. It just didn't seem fair.

Being in the Movies

A couple of days later when I was feeling at my lowest David and Marjorie took pity on me. They invited me to go out to Bamberton with them so that I could see where the movie was being made. To get there the bus climbed the Malahat and then took a sharp right turn before the Mill Bay turnoff. Then it followed a bumpy dirt road to a cement factory with a huge chimney. We had arrived at Bamberton At first it looked boring but then I saw a sight that made me gasp. It was a complete Norwegian village with a church, a community hall and several cottages all with sod roofs, white fronts and window boxes filled with flowers. It was beautiful.

In front of the community hall was a raised platform. David and Marjorie were there. They had donned their Norwegian costumes and were receiving dance instructions along with several other blonde children. David looked self-conscious with his white shirt buttoned at the neck, but Marjorie was obviously pleased with the flowered blouse she was wearing. Without any warning a Norwegian folk song blared out of a loudspeaker and the children began to dance. Hop, bob, jiggle, curtsey. It all looked ridiculous to me, but at least they were being paid well. After the cameraman finished filming the dance scene the children ran off-stage and I had an opportunity to explore the village. Every building I entered was the same. There was a door but nothing inside once the door was opened. All the pretty building fronts were held up by plywood and two-by-fours. The whole thing was a fake.

After my day at Bamberton I didn't feel so badly about not being in the movie. I wouldn't have wanted to spend the whole day bobbing up and down doing Norwegian folk dances. Even for a dollar a day.

David always had a funny tale to tell after he came home from filming.

"You should have seen Paul Muni today," David began.

Paul Muni was the star with the lead role.

"When he's not acting he spends all his time in front of a mirror. First he combs his hair and then he presses his finger against the wave to make his hair look just perfect. And then he takes an eye-liner and presses it into the corners of his eyes to make himself look really serious. Like this."

David pulled his face into what he believed was a serious expression.

"He's supposed to look serious because he's worried about all the people the Germans are executing in the village.

"I know you don't look Norwegian enough to be in the movie but you should see Paul Muni. He's short and dark and sneaky looking. He looks more like an Italian gangster than a Norwegian. He finds out that the Germans are building a big air-base just outside the village, so he escapes in a boat in the middle of the night. He wants to tell the British so they can send Commandos to destroy the base. But once he gets to England he falls in love with Anna Lee. She's a movie star too. That slows everything down and you wonder if he's ever going to get down to business with the Commandos. He's turned all soppy. And why would he fall in love with Anna Lee anyway? It's not like she's a glamour girl. They should have put Rita Hayworth in the movie.

"The best actor is Alexander Knox. He plays the German Commandant. He makes all the men in the village stand under the swastika flag while he shouts at them. Then they all have to yell "Heil Hitler". If they don't they get taken away and shot. He's not allowed to yell at us though 'cause we're just children. We don't get shot either."

Auntie Bea loved to hear David gossip about the movie and the actors. David kept her giggling the whole time. Then one evening at the dinner table Auntie Bea had a story of her own. She had been having tea at the Empress Hotel when Alexander Knox had marched in with several actors dressed as German soldiers. They had missed their bus ride to Bamberton.

"They marched right through the Empress at tea-time. Then they started doing the goose-step. Some of the old ladies thought they were real German soldiers and that we had been invaded. I actually saw Mabel Phipps have a coughing fit and fall out of her chair. She must have had a heart attack right there in the Empress."

Auntie Bea giggled all the way through her story. She had stolen the spotlight from David and had us all in hysterics when she described the terrified dowagers dropping their teacups at the Empress.

By the end of summer the filming had ended, and I was itching to see the finished movie. I wanted to see the part where the German soldiers shot the villagers. Then I could hiss at the Germans because they were so evil. And of course I wanted to see the part where the Commandos landed and blew up all the German planes.

But before the movie was released my life in Victoria took an unexpected turn. My mother, Elizabeth and I moved out of the Admirals House and into a home of our own.

## CHAPTER 12

## OAK BAY

Our new home was a small bungalow in Oak Bay. 1025 Monterey Avenue. I was ecstatic. I no longer had to share a bedroom with David. The afternoon sun shone on our new home and I was happy to just stand on the sidewalk soaking up the sunshine. I loved Oak Bay immediately. The Dockyard had been dark and gloomy but Oak Bay was bright and filled with light. There were people on the streets and I could walk wherever I wanted. Best of all there would be no hour-long streetcar ride home after school.

Elizabeth grumbled at first. In the Dockyard she had been allowed to collect eggs from the chickens every day. Here there were no chickens, but she quickly discovered that she could make hopscotch squares with chalk on the sidewalk and she soon forgot about the chickens. She made friends with a girl who lived on the other side of the street. Her name was Angela Brompton and she played hopscotch with Elizabeth on sunny afternoons. They invited me to join them but of course I refused. What would our new neighbours think if they saw me playing hopscotch with two little girls? When they tired of hopscotch they skipped and sang nursery rhymes. That was when I went indoors to work on my stamp album.

I may not have had to put up with David as a room-mate but now I had to share a bedroom with my mother and Elizabeth as our bungalow had only one bedroom. I had to sleep on a cot. I was embarrassed that I had to share with them, and when I dressed in the mornings I made sure my back was turned towards them.

Fortunately my mother soon found us a different place to live, a large grey duplex just a block up the street. 1155 Monterey Avenue. At last I had my very own bedroom. Right beside our side of the house was a large grove of oak trees and a smaller grove of laurel bushes where Elizabeth and I could hide from each other. I couldn't have been happier. I felt exactly the same way that I had when we spent the previous summer on the farm. I felt warm and free.

As soon as we were settled into 1155 my mother announced that my father was coming out from England and had a job waiting for him at Yarrows Shipyard in Esquimalt. We were to be one happy family just as we were at Sunny Corner in Reading.

My feelings were mixed. For one thing I was worried about him arriving safely. Every day the Colonist had news of ships that had been torpedoed by U-boats in the Atlantic. What if my father were to go down with one of those ships? Why couldn't he have waited until it was safer? And would we really be one happy family? My parents had fought about religion when we were living in Reading. I couldn't see any reason why they would get along any more peaceably here. My mother had failed to send me to Catechism after I complained about Father O'Reilly's bad breath. My father would be angry with her for not sending me and with me for not following my Catholic duty.

What about my independence? None of my friends at school had fathers at home, and now I was going to have a father to boss me. And anyway I had a nice relationship with my father just the way things were. I had been sending him letters with my drawings of ships and tanks and fighter planes, and he had been writing to me about the garden and the thieving rabbits and the birds that came to eat the suet he put out for them. Now there would be no more letters in brown envelopes addressed to Master John Napier-Hemy.

On the other hand the thought of having a father at home was comforting. Perhaps he would smoke Sweet Caporal cigarettes and give me the packages with the airplane pictures on the back. Perhaps he would increase my allowance. Perhaps he would help me set up my new bedroom and buy me materials for making model airplanes. Well, I would just have to wait and see.

In the meantime I was enjoying my new home. The oak grove was perfect for launching the little cardboard gliders that I bought with my allowance at Pomeroy's store at the foot of Newport Avenue. I even liked the girl who lived in the other side of the duplex. Her name was Minnie and she liked to climb up on the roof or play hide-and-seek with Elizabeth and myself in the laurel bushes. My mother said she was a tomboy. Somehow that made it fine for me to play with her and not worry about whether playing with a girl would turn me into a sissy. I teased her by making up rhymes like "Skinny Minnie in the garbage tinnie". She enjoyed being teased and asked me to make up more rhymes.

After Labour Day Elizabeth began school. She was enrolled in Kindergarten at a school called St. Christophers. She had a brand new uniform consisting of a white blouse, a brown and yellow striped tie, a brown coat and a brown bowler hat. My mother walked her to school every morning.

I teased her. "Is St. Christophers a real school? I'll bet you just play hopscotch all day."

Elizabeth just smiled and ignored me so I gave up trying to irritate her and went about my business.

One afternoon shortly after I had returned from school my father showed up at the front door. Just like that! I don't know how he found the way to our house. All I can recall is that he just mysteriously appeared. Perhaps this was his way of surprising us. When I first saw him I was shocked. He looked so old and shaky. What had happened to him? Had he been bombed in Reading? Had a U-boat fired torpedoes at his ship? He looked as though he had been through some terrible ordeal.

"Hello, Daddy," I ventured.

"Hello, Daddy," from Elizabeth.

My mother had a huge smile. "Thank goodness you made it safely," she said as she embraced him.

"It's so wonderful to be back with you all again," my father said. "The trip felt as though it was going to take forever. I love the home you've chosen for us. It's just the way you described it."

He was trembling, but I could see that it was from relief and from the joy of seeing us. He returned my mother's embrace, and then he hugged Elizabeth and myself. Elizabeth was small enough that he could lift her into the air. Then he reached inside his jacket pocket and pulled out a silver cigarette case.

It would be hard to describe my relief. My father had made it safely across the Atlantic and my mother had greeted him warmly. We were going to be a happy family of four with a home of our own.

"Hubert, you look so thin and tired," my mother said. "I'm going to have to build you up."

That meant porridge and lots of it. *Quaker Oats* or *Cream of Wheat* or *Sunny Boy* for a special treat. I hated the *Cream of*

*Wheat* because my mother cooked it too quickly and it usually had lumps in it. *Sunny Boy* was fine because it didn't lump. We had to be careful with the sugar because it was rationed, but there was always plenty of milk. Every so often she would let up on the porridge and give us *Corn Flakes* or *Rice Krispies* with toast. I liked the *Rice Krispies* because they really did go "Pop, Crackle, Snap" just like the picture on the cereal box said they would, but you had to eat them quickly or they would go soggy. There was no butter for the toast but we did have something called apple butter that was made from mushed-up apples.

After breakfast my mother made my father a big sandwich lunch that she tucked into a metal lunch-box for him to carry on the streetcar when he went to Yarrows in the morning. He started work right away without taking a holiday first. He was urgently needed at Yarrows where they were building corvettes and frigates to help make the Atlantic safe for the convoys to Britain.

Our reunion went well. My father seemed more relaxed and smiled more often and my mother seemed to be pleased with her efforts in "building him up". So far so good. Our family seemed pretty much the way I thought a family should be. There was no arguing about religion.

Not yet anyway.

My father licked me into spiritual shape pretty quickly. He was, as I had anticipated, seriously concerned about the state of my soul. He began by insisting that I go to Mass every Sunday. To miss Mass was a mortal sin and he certainly didn't want it on his conscience if I had to spend eternity in Hell through his negligence. The two of us began walking all the way from Monterey Avenue to St. Patrick's Church on Haultain Street.

I hated the walk. No lovely little cottage gardens, just a boring walk through a boring neighbourhood with squat stuccoed bungalows, picket fences with peeling white paint, grass coming up through the cracks in the sidewalk and the occasional unkempt dog. It took 45 minutes altogether but it always seemed much longer.

My father pointed out that failing to attend Mass had placed my immortal soul in danger. If I were to drop dead right now on our way to church my soul would go straight to Hell. I looked up at an ominous grey sky and wondered if God was preparing a thunderbolt for me especially. Even if I had only committed a venial sin I could expect to spend an unimaginable time in Purgatory waiting for my soul to be thoroughly cleansed. I began walking faster so that I could reach the Confessional as soon as possible. I noticed that my father was falling behind and starting to wheeze, so I had to slow down again.

Once inside the church I headed straight for the Confessional where the priest was hidden from me on the other side of a metal grating. What did he look like? I had no idea. Would he have foul breath like Father O'Malley in Esquimalt? He didn't. A huge relief because I could be close to him without gagging.

"Father, I have committed a mortal sin." There was a rustle of cloth on the other side and a slight nasal moan. I had expected shock but what came out sounded more like boredom as though I had interrupted him in the middle of a good book.

"Yes, my son?"

"I have missed Mass on many occasions."

"Hmmm. Willfully?"

"I don't think so. My mother didn't send me and my father was in England. My mother's not Catholic."

"Anything else?"

"I have been deceitful."

"Deceitful?"

"I think so. I mean, I could have gone to Mass on my own but I pretended that I needed an adult to send me."

"Understandable, but you have to say a Penance. One "Our Father" and five "Hail Mary's".

"For being deceitful?"

"No, that's for everything. Go in peace and sin no more."

## Oak Bay

What a relief! I thought my Penance was going to take several days. In actual fact I had finished the final Hail Mary just before Mass started, so I was able to sit through Mass with a clear conscience. My father must have left the church with a clear conscience as well. There was no more talk of eternal torments. Instead he talked about the wonderful things we could do together like renting a rowboat from the Oak Bay Boathouse and rowing out to Jimmy Chicken Island. Or fly-fishing on the Cowichan River. These activities sounded like fun, but I wasn't so sure that I wanted to do them. I had been my own boss for almost three years, and I valued my independence. Besides I was afraid that my father would begin one of his gloomy talks again once we were on our own.

My mother wasn't too interested in my father's thoughts or plans but she was certainly concerned about the state of his health. He looked so thin, so worn and so worried. Every time he did a chore around the house he got out of breath. She was determined to restore his health with good food. More healthy porridges in the morning. Spam and apple butter sandwiches in his lunch kit and hot, steaming dinners when he came home. Dinners usually consisted of macaroni cheese or scrambled eggs, boiled potatoes, peas and carrots or turnip boiled into some kind of a mush. On the weekends she usually had enough coupons in her ration book to buy some ground beef for a meatloaf. Occasionally there was enough meat for a stew, but she usually spoiled the stews by adding in huge chunks of carrot. On Friday we had boiled cod or haddock. We were not supposed to complain because, as my father pointed out, people in England were eating sausages made from sawdust.

"And standing in line in the cold for them!" he added.

Then there were the desserts. There was a thick steamy custard which always had a layer of skin on the top. We were allowed to peel back the skin before we started, but then we had to eat the skin when we got to the bottom of the bowl. Nothing was to be wasted. There was chocolate pudding that was made in exactly the same way and never really tasted like chocolate. There was rice pudding, bread pudding, tapioca pudding and cream of tapioca for a special treat on Sundays. There was a wobbly white pudding called junket that came out of a white packet with *"Rennie's Junket"* on the label. There was Jello which came out of a coloured packet, a yellow packet for Lemon Jello, a red packet for Strawberry Jello and so on, but they all tasted pretty much the same.

The very worst dessert was called blancmange. The word was French and it meant "something white to eat". My mother made it with powdered milk and cornstarch. When it cooled it had a bluish underlay and when you took a spoonful it had lumps in it just like the lumps in *Cream of Wheat*. It looked disgusting and tasted horrible, but if we were lucky my mother would scoop a little treacle or molasses onto the top. It was exactly like the blancmange that Matron made at school. Perhaps my mother had gone to Glenlyon and asked Matron for her secret recipe.

If we had apples my mother baked them. I helped my mother core them and that way I was able to make sure there weren't any pips or pieces of core left behind to spoil my enjoyment. If we had a little sugar left over my mother would sprinkle it on the apples before they went in the oven. When the sugar melted over the tough skins it was a bit like toffee. I liked baked apples better than puddings.

The least objectionable pudding was called "Camel's Hump". It was a baked light brown doughy pudding that looked like a camel's hump after it was taken out of the oven and turned upside down on a plate. If my mother had some cooking dates on hand they would go into the dough to liven it up a little. There was a variation of *Camel's Hump* she sometimes made with raisins or currants. That was called *Spotted Dick*.

Once my mother tried making a dessert called trifle. She made if with layers of Jello, custard, stale cake and a dollop of damson jam. The Jello sort of melded into the cake on one side and the custard made the cake soggy on the other side. I came perilously close to throwing up after a couple of bites so my mother didn't make it again..

There was always plenty of milk and powdered stuff for making puddings, and my father never tired of telling us how lucky we were.

"I'm already feeling better, Winifred, with you making these wonderful desserts."

"Just what you need to build you up, Hubert. You're starting to look better."

I thought my father was looking better too, and if the puddings were responsible, well, I had better just keep quiet. I didn't want to sound like a spoiled Canadian brat by complaining. But it would have been so nice if we could have had roast quail once in a while like we did in the Dockyard.

My father was looking better, and my mother seemed satisfied with the results, but something was wrong. There was tension in the air. It started to show one Sunday morning when my father gulped his tea so he could make "a good headstart" getting away to Mass.

"Aren't you going to finish your tea, Hubert? And I've made extra toast. I thought you'd enjoy that on your day off."

"I'd love to stay, but I really do have to get going. It's a long walk to church."

Nothing more was said but I noticed my mother giving my father a sharp look, and I could see his brow furrowing with anxiety.

A few more Sundays and the hostilities began to come out in the open. My mother had failed to keep her promise to send me to Catechism. And what about my First Communion? She was supposed to see that I was prepared for it, and I wasn't. I could easily have taken it at the church in Esquimalt, but nothing had happened.

*"But, Daddy; you should have smelled the priest's breath,"* I thought, but I didn't say it out loud.

My mother let it be known that she was fed up with all this religiosity. Her father had never gone to church unless it was Christmas or Easter, but he still managed to be a fine person. He was kind to others, looked after his garden, and helped out family members when they were in financial trouble.

"Just like he helped us during the Depression, Hubert. Do you think you're better than he was just because you go to church all the time?"

The war had resumed and my instinct was to keep my head down to avoid the crossfire. Some Sunday mornings I stuck my head under my eiderdown and feigned illness. In the afternoon I would come downstairs in my dressing gown looking as pale and fragile as I possibly could. Both of my parents fell for it. They had almost lost me to pneumonia while we were in England, and they didn't want a repeat performance. My mother made me *Oxo* or *Bovril* and made sure that I was warmly dressed and stayed indoors.

"You're not to catch a chill. You know how delicate you are!"

My father seemed satisfied with the excuses, and set out for church on his own, presumably with a clear conscience for having done his best. I always returned to church the following week, went to Confession and confessed to being "deceitful". Which was true. I was deceitful and becoming more so all the time.

The priest couldn't have been all that interested in my deceptions. There was always a lineup at the Confessional and he liked to start Mass punctually at 11 a.m.

"One *Our Father* and three *Hail Mary's*" and I was sent on my way.

Walking home from school in September was way better than taking the streetcar to the Dockyard. I usually walked home with Bill Carrington and Rod Peary. We walked along the Beach Drive seawall and stopped to identify ducks. When we tired of ducks we piled onto an old-fashioned swing on the opposite side of the road from the Dorchester Apartments. We quickly worked up an appetite on the swings and headed for Pomeroy's store at the foot of Newport Avenue. If we had any pennies we pooled them and bought a Pep-Chew or a Nickel Lunch. Then we continued along Windsor Road past Windsor Park until we reached Transit Road. That was where Bill and Rod lived with Mrs. Carrington and Bill's younger sister, Janet. Mrs. Carrington was as kind as her son and always made sure that I had a glass of milk or a cookie before I continued on my homeward journey to Monterey Avenue.

Shortly after school started we were joined by two new boys, Hughie and Jamie Cray. They were from Texas and their father was away in the Navy somewhere. They had moved with their mother into one of the apartments opposite Pomeroy's store. Hughie was the older of the two and was called *Cray 1* at school even though he was smaller than Jamie who was called *Cray 2*. I especially like Hughie because he was almost as small as I was, and I felt more normal when I was with him.

Five was way more fun than three especially when we all stormed into Pomeroy's Store at once. For one thing we had more money when we pooled it together and that increased the number of possibilities among the jellies, jawbreakers. licorice, *Pep-Chew, Nickel Lunch* and *Macintosh's Toffee*. But then of course we had to divide our loot five ways so we were really not that much farther ahead. We needed a strategy. Bill went up to Mr. and Mrs. Pomeroy and started talking to them. I don't know what he said but he seemed to have a way of charming them.

"Such a nice boy," they must have thought. "So well-behaved. So well brought-up." But while Bill was chatting to them Rod was slipping one or two *Nickel Lunches* or *Pep-Chews* into his jacket pocket. Never too many because he didn't want them to catch on that anything was missing. That little bit of trickery meant that we walked out with a more substantial haul. Both the *Nickel Lunch* and *Pep-Chew* were pathetic, a pale imitation of real chocolate bars. All the *Nickel Lunch* consisted of was a Graham wafer with the chocolate spread on to it so thinly that you could see right through to the wafer. *Pep-Chew* had an equally thin layer of chocolate which covered some peppermint–flavoured sticky stuff which got caught in your teeth, took forever to dissolve, and didn't taste all that good anyway

If it was a cold day we snuck out a *Macintosh's Toffee*. If you exposed it to the cold for a few minutes it got hard enough to crack into pieces on a stone. If it was too warm it was just a hopeless sticky mess that couldn't be divided. We were always thankful for what we got. We knew that if we were in England or occupied Europe there wouldn't be anything sweet at all. The Pomeroys never caught on and we were always welcome in their store.

After Mrs. Carrington had given me a glass of milk and a cookie I thanked her and headed for home. Now I was on my own and I had to walk along Windsor Road from Transit Road. St. David Street, St. Patrick Street, Oliver Street, Monterey Avenue and then I was home. I walked home with a clear conscience. It never occurred to me that eating stolen candy might be a venial sin. After all it was Rod Peary who had stolen the candy and not me.

I had other worries though. My route intersected with the route taken by several of the Monterey School pupils on their way home. Monterey School was a public school. Boys and girls without school uniforms. Boys with corduroy pants, sweaters and windbreakers. As I feared – one day a solitary small boy with a school uniform and a satchel proved too tempting a target for two public school ruffians – one large boy with an unruly thatch of black hair and a scowl – one slightly smaller boy with slicked back dirty blonde hair and a sneer.

"Hey, squirt."

"Hey, goody-good. Private school. Want to fight?"

"No, I don't." In my anxiety I blinked at them several times.

"Hey, Blinky. Put down your satchel and fight!"

"No."

"Sissy!"

As they lunged forward I grabbed a huge clod of loose dirt and grass from the ditch, threw it at them, and raced home. I was fast enough to outrun them. After that incident I always looked carefully around me between Transit Road and Monterey Avenue. I had been identified as a coward and would be fair game for the two bullies if they spotted me again.

I didn't tell my parents about my encounter, but my father must have sensed that my size and slight build were worrying me. One day he brought out a book written by a man named Herr Mueller. It was a body-building book and the idea was that I was to stand in front of my dresser mirror in my undershorts with the book close by and follow the arrows that would show me how to raise my arms, bend my torso and so on.

It pleased me to learn that my father was interested in the state of my body and not just my soul. But I didn't like the fact that Herr Mueller was a German. I knew a little bit about the German obsession with physical activity and where it had taken them, but I decided that I could probably do the exercises without turning into a Nazi. Maybe Mueller was a good German, and I did need to be strong if I ever had to fight one of the Monterey School bullies.

After a few weeks I imagined that the exercises were helping me. I was admiring my progress in the mirror when my father walked in behind me. I was anticipating that he would be pleased with my efforts.

"You seem to be coming along quite nicely. But beware of self-idolatry. I can lead you into sin."

"Okay."

## Oak Bay

But sin? What sin? I had no idea what he was talking about. I had never heard of self-idolatry before. The next day when I started my exercises I didn't feel the same way about them. I felt a sense of shame as though I was doing something dirty. I stopped the exercises, put Herr Mueller's book away and never brought it out again. Maybe if I just let nature take its course I would start to grow and develop anyway.

Elizabeth must have sensed my confusion. One morning she came running out of her bedroom and into the upstairs hall in her underwear. She was waggling a pencil between her legs and pretending it was a penis. Not only that she was laughing.

"Don't be rude!" I shouted.

Then I smacked the pencil out of her hand. She burst into tears.

"I'm sorry," I said. But she kept on sobbing.

I felt terrible. I was a bully. No better than the two boys from Monterey School who had wanted me to fight. And I felt shame. Shame about my body and now I had transferred that shame onto my sister. That made me a prig as well as a bully. I wished I could undo the harm I had caused her, but there was no turning back or making amends. I had tainted my relationship with her.

I hated the way I felt and I was confused about my father. Why had he been so keen about Mueller's exercises and then become uncomfortable when I was doing so well with them? None of my friends at school had fathers on the scene approving or disapproving of whatever they did. I didn't wish for one instant that my father was back in England with the Germans dropping bombs on him, but it did complicate my life having two parents in charge of my life instead of only one.

It was the same every Sunday at Saint Patrick's Church on Haultain Street. The people who had made Confessions proceeded to the Communion Rail. There they waited for the priest and the two altar boys to make their appearance. The priest carried a big silver cup and one of the altar boys carried a silver tray with wafers on it. Then the priest took one of the wafers from the silver tray, leaned over the rail and placed a wafer on the outstretched tongue of each penitent. It looked a little undignified. Then he held out the silver cup and each penitent took a sip of the wine to wash down the wafer. I assumed that God had eliminated any germs that might be present.

After this was over the penitents returned to their pews where the rest of us were waiting for Mass to start. But I wasn't allowed to take part. because I had never taken my First Communion. The reason I had never taken my First Communion was that I hadn't been confirmed. And the reason I hadn't been confirmed was that I had been too sick in England to go to my Confirmation. And the reason I hadn't been confirmed in Victoria was because my mother had failed to send me to Catechism at the Catholic Church in Esquimalt. The building blocks just weren't there, and that was what set me apart from the rest of the congregation and why I had to sit glumly in my pew watching it all happen. I felt isolated.

But there were a couple of things that made me feel a little less isolated. In the pew directly behind us was a man named John Hart. He was the Liberal Premier of British Columbia.. So there, Anglicans! The most important man in the whole province was right here with me in this church. The other thing was the incense. At a certain point in the Mass the priest and the altar boys marched slowly down the centre aisle swinging a metal ball which hung from a long chain. Inside the metal ball there was burning incense, and as the priest swung his arm the scent of incense wafted out over the whole congregation. I liked the smell and I felt at this moment that I was being included and treated equally.

On the way home my father explained what happened when people took Communion. It was all about a miracle called "transubstantiation". The wafers were the Body of Christ and the wine was the Blood of Christ.

"During Communion the wafer *is* the body of Christ. It doesn't just represent the body of Christ. It really is the body of Christ."

*"That's fine,"* I thought. *"That's what the wafers are."*

"And the wine is the blood of Christ. It's a miracle."

I think my father thought I should have difficulty believing the miracle of transubstantiation. But I didn't. It seemed quite reasonable.

"You have to have Faith," my father continued. "It's a miracle, and you have to have Faith to believe it."

But why did my father think it should be so difficult for me to believe? Did he think I was stupid? My father must have mistaken my silence for doubt, so I had to listen to the explanation again the following Sunday. And the Sunday after that.

"Communion is a sacrament. It's the sacrament of Eucharist. And when you take Communion you are taking part in that sacrament. It's a special gift of God to Man. When you take Communion you are in a state of grace. That's why I want to have you confirmed."

That was the part I didn't understand. How could I know what a state of grace was like if I hadn't experienced it? It was easier just to think about wafers and wine. At least I could see them. But I didn't ask my father to explain it any further. The truth was that I didn't really want to know, and it would have tired me to hear the explanation one more time. Once each Sunday was enough.

The walk home took us across the Oak Bay High School grounds and then to the bridge that forded Bowker Creek.

We always took this route home because my father would have a full bladder after Mass and he was able to pee into the bushes beside Bowker Creek without being seen. The mouth of Bowker Creek was right beside Glenlyon School.

I wondered if my father's pee was finding its way to the part of the beach where I liked to play at recess. I looked up at the clouds while I waited for my father to finish.

"Protestants don't believe in miracles. They don't believe in anything much. Your mother's father spent every Sunday morning gardening. I suppose gardening was his religion."

I didn't want to hear this. Although I had only been four years old when I last saw my grandfather he had a special place in my heart. I probably didn't really remember him but I had a photograph of him and I clung to a myth that he was a kind, loving person.

I knew that gardening wasn't a religion and I didn't want to hear from anyone that he was foolish enough to believe that it was.

My father wanted me confirmed. It wasn't too late for that. I wanted to be confirmed too so that I wouldn't feel so isolated every Sunday. I wanted to fit in with the congregation and take my rightful place at the Communion rail. My mother did not want me confirmed. The last time I had prepared for Confirmation I had become ill, and she didn't want me getting sick again. That didn't seem logical. It seemed to me that she was creating a phony argument so that I could be kept away from being confirmed. How could preparing for my First Communion possibly make me sick? Bored perhaps but not sick

I didn't say anything. It was up to my parents to come to some sort of agreement. But they never did. They couldn't because they were both right, or so they thought. Every Sunday my mother became more and more furious with my father. My father became more and more abject and despondent, and I became more inward and depressed. If miracles were possible, this was where one was required. If God could do a big miracle like transubstantiation for millions of Catholics he could surely do a small one with my parents. But the miracle never came.

The struggle showed in my parents' faces. My mother developed tight, pursed lips, a frown that could shatter glass and a terrifying high-pitched scream. My father's brow was creased with worry lines. He became tearful in the face of my mother's rage. He even got down on his knees and pleaded with her. Nothing changed. They both became more and more scarred by a conflict I couldn't fathom.

*"My father shouldn't plead with my mother,"* I thought. *"He should get off his knees and smack her. That would make her stop screaming."*

My mother's rage frightened me and I wanted to be protected. I'm not sure where I got the idea that my father should hit my mother when she behaved like this, but that was what I thought. My parents never did hit one another. They just carried on with my mother shouting and my father pleading.

What made matters even worse was that my father would talk about the feud on the way to church.

"Your mother promised me she would become a Catholic after we married. She never did. She promised me she would send you to Mass when she came out to Canada with you and Elizabeth. She didn't.

"God will judge me harshly for all this. I promised God that I would convert your mother to Catholicism. I haven't been able to do that. I promised God I would raise my children as Catholics. I haven't managed to have you confirmed, and Elizabeth is being raised as an Anglican. My failures have placed my soul in danger."

That sounded silly to me. I couldn't believe that my father's soul was in danger. After all, he had tried his best and surely God was reasonable. What hurt me was not my father's supposed failure but the fact that he was talking about my mother in this way. As much as I was frightened by my mother's temper and harshness, it hurt me even more to hear my father running her down. She was my mother after all, and I wanted to be loyal. She was the one who had looked after me all through the war, not my father.

Oak Bay

I wanted to tell my father that I didn't like him talking about my mother. I thought he should have kept it to himself and not load it onto my shoulders, but I couldn't say anything. I was sure that if I did he would just carry on telling me how sinful he was.

And I couldn't tell my mother that I didn't like her screaming either. She would probably have started screaming at me too if I had. I couldn't talk to either of them, and there was no-one else I could talk to. My school friends were all Anglicans and wouldn't have understood. So I kept it all inside. Sometimes I felt as though I would explode.

By Sunday evening the storm had subsided. Once a month my parents combined their ration coupons and bought a roast of beef. My mother cooked it to perfection with rare meat on the inside and nice crispy fat on the outside. There were roast potatoes, dark brown and hard on the outside and soft and steamy on the inside, Yorkshire pudding with gravy and runner beans. Then they seemed to enjoy each other's company and I enjoyed my dinner. For a wonderful couple of hours all was right with the world. It wasn't a miracle but it was the next best thing.

CHAPTER *13*

# BUILDING AIRPLANES

While my parents fought and I worried about the state of my soul, I managed to escape from the gloomiest of my thoughts. When my father came out from England he brought a radio with him. It was the very same radio that I had coveted years before in Granny Hemy's apartment in London. I had felt guilty about this radio because I had always hoped we could have it when Granny Hemy died. But she had died before the war broke out and my father had kept the radio with him in Reading so I didn't have to feel guilty about it any more. Now I could enjoy the radio when I came home from school and before my father came home for dinner.

Every afternoon I rushed upstairs and turned on the radio in time for *Jack Armstrong, the All-American Boy.* Jack Armstrong was a high school boy who flew everywhere with his Uncle Jim and his friends, Billy and Betty Fairchild. They went to exciting and dangerous places where no-one else could go. If there were German spies building a secret base in the headwaters of the Amazon, Jack Armstrong would find them. If the Flying Tigers were flying dangerous missions over Burma Jack Armstrong would be there crouched behind the pilot of a P-40 who was shooting down Japanese Zeroes. At the end of 15 minutes he would be left in a dire predicament. If the P-40 were going down in flames he would be parachuting into a dangerous jungle swarming with Japanese troops. If you wanted to know what was going to happen next, you had to tune in the next day. If you sent in a boxtop from Wheaties and a dime Jack Armstrong would send you a special secret gift. The only problem was that Wheaties were only sold in the U.S.A.

After the Wheaties commercial there was a pause followed by "The Flight of the Bumblebee" playing in the background. This was the signal that the *Green Hornet* was about to begin solving mysteries with the aid of his faithful Oriental servant Kato.

After they had finished with the next phase of their important work there was more music. This time it was the "William Tell Overture". The first bars conjured up a mental image of the *Lone Ranger and Tonto* out on the American desert hunting down cattle rustlers and train robbers. I found the program a little boring because cattle rustlers didn't really compare with Japs or Nazis as villains.

The Lone Ranger was followed by *Batman and Robin*. The scene shifted from the desert to a big American city called Gotham, where the caped crusaders tracked down gangsters in the middle of the night. Best of all they scooped up Nazi saboteurs who were about to blow up a bridge or a power plant. The Nazis were always disguised as American civilians, but they gave themselves away when they made the mistake of saying "Ja" instead of "Yes".

The Green Hornet, Lone Ranger and Batman were okay, but if I missed Jack Armstrong for any reason it spoiled my day. I hated not finding out how he escaped from his many predicaments.

Then my father came home from Yarrows and we shared the radio so that we could hear the BBC World News at 6 p.m. The BBC announcer was grave but reassuring. I always felt at the end of the News that the Allies would prevail and that the world was going to be saved from the Axis dictatorships.

Another thing my father had brought with him from England was a huge wooden box with drawers that stuck when you tried to open them. The box was filled with wrenches of all sizes and descriptions. My father was a marine engineer. He must have been a good one because he knew what every wrench was for. That was why Yarrows wanted him in Victoria to help build warships.

He pulled out an odd-looking wrench with a small head and a long handle.

"I used this one when I first sailed with the Merchant Marine in the Mediterranean. It was the only tool that would reach between the steam boiler and the bulkhead."

## Building Airplanes

"Wow!" I replied, but I was already tuning out. I couldn't think of anything more boring and dirty than tightening a bolt in the engine room of a ship. He went on to explain the uses of the other wrenches but he was wasting his time with me. It was like hearing about transubstantiation, the Trinity or the Immaculate Conception. It made some kind of sense but it wasn't interesting. My head was in the sky with Jack Armstrong shooting down Zeroes or Me-109s.

Having a father in my life was much more satisfying when he brought home interesting scraps for me from Yarrows Shipyards. First he brought home pieces of white pine and then he bought me an Xacto knife, a tube of airplane glue and some pieces of sandpaper. Then I bought a copy of Mechanix Illustrated with my own allowance so I could have plans for building model planes. I cleared a space in my bedroom and went to work. Once I had completed a Spitfire and a Me-109 I carried out dogfights in my bedroom while I listened to Jack Armstrong.

"Nyaah! Nyaah! Pfff! Pfff! Pfff! Nyaah! Pkooh!" The Me-109 hurtled to earth and crashed in a farmer's field with its evil pilot trapped inside.

The Spitfire was difficult. The curve of the wings had to be absolutely right or it didn't look like a Spitfire. But when I finally got it right I was infatuated. What a beautiful plane! How I wanted to be a Spitfire pilot and fly one of these lovely machines in an attack on a German bomber formation while

Me-109s came after me like a flight of hornets. Even if I were shot down and killed there would be a photograph of me in the newspapers.

After I had mastered the small wooden models I moved on to larger models that were supposed to fly. They came in kits with a picture of the plane in flight after being released from the hands of a boy like myself. They were difficult to assemble. You had to make templates out of pieces of cardboard and then carefully align long stringers of wood that you inserted into the templates to make the fuselage. This was a painstaking piece of work. One stringer out of place and the whole fuselage would be warped. The wings and tail were made the same way and then glued onto the fuselage.

The next step was to glue tissue paper to the skeletal plane and make the whole thing taut by painting on banana oil.

Then, if you wanted to make it fly, which of course I did, you glued a hook into the tail, a hook onto the propeller and joined the two hooks with an elastic band that you had dipped into glycerine. The glycerine was supposed to keep the elastic supple so that it wouldn't break in mid-flight.

The final step was to glue decals onto the wings and tail, a red, white and blue bulls-eye for a British plane, a red star for a Russian one and so on. Then your plane was ready for action. To make it fly you twisted the propeller around and around to place tension on the elastic. When you released the propeller and the plane simultaneously it was supposed to fly.

There were problems. The templates were made of cardboard instead of balsa wood because all the balsa trees from South America were being cut down to make life rafts. The stringers were made of cheap pine that snapped easily. The elastics were made of some synthetic product because all the real rubber from the Amazon had gone into making airplane tires. The banana oil never really dried. This meant that if you hung the model from the ceiling of your room it soon became covered with dust. But there was a war on, and you just had to be content with the materials available.

Despite these obstacles I was ambitious. I wanted to build a German Stuka divebomber. It was the most difficult plane I could have chosen because of the gull wings.

When Christmas rolled around I was happy to be part of a whole family, especially when we went to Uncle Jim and Auntie Clara's cocktail party. Uncle Jim had a superior way of looking at my mother, and I felt that if my father was beside her Uncle Jim would show her a little more respect. I also felt that we would be on more of an equal footing with the Beech family now that we were a complete family just like they were.

As usual Uncle Jim had tacked a huge artificial wreath replete with golden balls and red satin bows to the front door. My father rang the doorbell and Uncle Jim opened it immediately. He must have been standing right behind the frosted glass pane beside the door and seen us walking up the steps.

"Waaal, Hubert, how are you? Welcome to Victoria. Wonderful you could be here this year. Come on in."

Uncle Jim blew a blast of cigar smoke into the frosty air and ushered us in. After he had taken our coats he pointed us in the direction of a large plate of hors d'oeuvres and a small glass table with a huge silver cigarette box on it. It looked just like my father's cigarette box except that it was twice as large.

"Just halp yourself, Hubert."

My father's eyes lit up. If there was one thing in life he enjoyed above all else it was smoking.

"Thank you, Jim. I must say that you and Clara have done a wonderful job of decorating your home."

My father was looking in the direction of a Christmas tree that was buried in gaudy ornaments.

"Waal, thanks. Just a few little things that Clara and I hauled out of the basement. Leftovers from last year. You can't buy decent ornaments any more with the war on."

That was as far as the conversation went. Uncle Jim's voice trailed off at the end of his last sentence. He inserted a toothpick in between two gold-filled teeth and moved towards the next guests. It was the Beech family.

"Waal, Roy. Good to see you. Sunk any Jap subs lately? Ha ha ha!"

Uncle Roy reddened and made his lips go tight. He moved on to the hors d'oeuvres tray without even answering. I knew what Uncle Jim was getting at. A Japanese submarine had recently fired two shells at the Estevan Point Lighthouse and then disappeared into the night before the Canadian Navy had a chance to pursue it. I thought it was rude of Uncle Jim to bring up the subject and disrespectful to Uncle Roy. Who did he think was protecting him and his fancy house anyway?

I spotted David immediately. I hadn't seen him all Fall because his parents had sent him away to a private school in Vancouver for some reason or other. He looked really grownup. He had grown a couple of inches and was wearing an expensive-looking navy blue blazer emblazoned with the crest of his new school. He came towards us, grinning from ear to ear, and shook my father's hand.

"Merry Christmas, Hubie!"

Hubie? Had David really called my father Hubie? This was my father, the man who had spoken to me about all the important matters of faith and salvation. And here was my teenaged cousin calling him Hubie. Cheeky! I waited for a wrathful God to shake a finger at him. But nothing happened. My father took it all in good grace.

"Merry Christmas, David. I must say you're looking really grownup."

I reflected on this interchange. Maybe my father needed a little teasing. Maybe he's been taking himself a bit too seriously.

"Come and say *hi* to Bea and Roy."

And what was this? Now he was calling his own parents Bea and Roy. Had he no respect for anyone? Here he was being cheeky to his father, Commodore Beech of the Royal Canadian Navy, and getting away with it.

I envied David. I knew that I could never talk to adults in that manner and get away with it. I didn't have the, what was it I didn't have? It was personality, or "poi-so-nal-i-ty" as David would have pronounced it. I would have simply made a fool of myself. Once again David had managed to make me feel like an ineffective little blob. How I wished that I could be as brash and self-confident as he was.

"Well, Shorty, are you going to see the movie?"

I could feel my cheeks flushing.

"Movie? What movie?"

"Come on, you know what movie. *Commandos Strike at Dawn* is what movie. It's coming out in the New Year. Something to see in '43."

"Wow, that's pretty exciting," I said.

I didn't want to give David the satisfaction of knowing how jealous I was and how much I resented him for being one of the extras. Then I stuffed one of Aunt Clara's sandwiches into my mouth and pretended to be fascinated with the Christmas tree.

We didn't stay at the cocktail party all that long. In fact we left at about the same time as the Beeches. We waited together for the Uplands streetcar. All the tension we had felt going into the party was dissipated. My mother and Auntie Bea started joking about all the people at the party, especially Uncle Jim and Auntie Clara. Then my father and Uncle Roy joined in and soon our combined families were in a complete uproar. Why, going to Uncle Jim's cocktail party was better than a trip to the circus. When we finally arrived home I was feeling pretty good about myself and my family. What a shame that we would have to wait another year for Uncle Jim's next cocktail party!

When we returned home it was time to open our presents. There was a large box under the tree with my name on it in my father's handwriting. I knew that I could expect something exciting now that my father was here organizing my presents. In my excitement I completely forgot how annoyed I felt with David. I unwrapped the box carefully. Good paper was not to be wasted. My present was better than anything I could have expected. It was a chemistry set!

I could hardly believe my eyes when I opened the box. It was filled with cylindrical wooden boxes, each one containing a different chemical. Not only that, there were test tubes, clamps for holding the test tubes, an alcohol burner with a wick and a tin of methyl hydrate to use in the burner. There was a set of instructions for various *experiments* I could perform myself. I could watch colours change as I combined chemicals. I could make popping sounds, turn liquids into colloids or crystals, create terrible smells and even manage a minor explosion or two. This would be way better than struggling with airplane models.

My mother must have read my mind.

"I'm not having you make any bad smells in the house. If you want to play with chemicals you'll have to do it in the basement. And be careful. I don't want you blowing yourself up or setting the house on fire."

*"Perfect!"* I thought. *"I'll be on my own down there and I'll be able to do anything I want."*

I went down to the basement and set up my laboratory as close to the furnace as I possibly could. It was cold down there and I wanted to stay as warm as possible. First I poured some of the methyl hydrate into the alcohol burner and watched the wick soak it up. When it was completely drenched I took a large kitchen match, struck it on the basement floor and lit the burner. There was a small metal knob that I could use to raise and lower the wick depending on how large a flame I wanted. The methyl hydrate burned clean and the flame had a lovely blue centre. As soon as I had the flame at the height I wanted I went straight to the instruction book to find an experiment that required heat. I was so excited that it never occurred to me that I should have chosen the experiment first and then decided whether or not I needed heat.

In my excitement I reached for a test tube and knocked over the burner. Flaming methyl hydrate spilled onto the floor. What was I to do? There was a large galvanized metal jug next to the sink where my mother soaked the laundry. I grabbed a jug, filled it with water, and poured the water onto the flames. That was how you put out a fire, wasn't it? You poured water onto it. Anyone knew that.

But that was absolutely the wrong thing to do. Instead of putting out the fire all the water did was to spread the burning methyl hydrate across the basement floor. Soon the fire was right at the base of one of the huge wooden posts supporting the floor above me. What if the post caught on fire? It could burn the whole house down. I should have rushed upstairs to tell my parents that there was an emergency. But I couldn't. I was too ashamed to admit to them how stupid I had been. I decided to wait instead.

As luck would have it the fire burned itself out before it had an opportunity to spread to the wooden post. Then I grabbed a mop and sopped up the water I had spilled onto the flames. There! Now there was no evidence to tell my parents how careless I had been. Should I tell the priest next Sunday that I had been deceitful? Was destroying evidence to pretend that nothing had happened a form of deceit? I wasn't quite sure.

I continued to use my chemistry set in the basement but with much greater care. For weeks I was haunted by images of our home going up in flames with my mother, father and Elizabeth trapped inside.

"Dad, do you think you could buy me a model kit for a Stuka dive bomber?"

I had decided to start calling my father Dad instead of Daddy because I thought Daddy sounded babyish.

"Wait until payday and I'll see if I have enough money left over."

I waited and the following week my father presented me with the kit. I was thrilled. In my mind's eye I had already completed this evil-looking machine which would be machine-gunning helpless French refugees until a Spitfire came along to blast it out of the sky.

The project was difficult but with the aid of my mother's used thread bobbins I was able to raise the wingtips up from

## Building Airplanes

my worktable so that the wings would tilt at exactly the right angle. Weeks later when I was finished it really did look like a Stuka dive bomber. I examined my workmanship from every possible angle and felt proud of what I had accomplished.

I couldn't wait to make it fly. I should have taken it to Windsor Park where there was plenty of room to send it soaring. But I was impatient. Instead of taking the model to the park I took it to the oak grove beside our duplex. If I aimed the model exactly right I should be able to miss the oak trees.

I wound up the propeller, aimed the Stuka at a gap between the trees and released it. It flew! It actually flew. I was ecstatic. It flew straight and true, just the way in was supposed to. But then as the elastic unwound the model lost power. It lurched uncertainly towards the ground where the wheels would surely protect it from crashing. That never happened. As it descended, it veered abruptly into the closest oak tree. I ran to pick it up from the ground and saw that one of the gull wings had been badly damaged.

I took it back to my bedroom and surveyed the damage. Some of the stringers inside the wing had cracked, and I found it impossible to restore the plane to its original shape. After I had repaired it as best as I could, I hung it from the ceiling. If I looked at it from a certain angle it still looked like a Stuka, but it was never quite right. It quickly accumulated

Building Airplanes

dust, and each day it looked a little worse. I finally assigned it to the garbage can and after a brief period of mourning I went on to the next project.

## CHAPTER 14

## AUNT MADGE'S HISTORY OF VICTORIA

"*The Commandos Strike at Dawn*" was released shortly after Christmas, and our whole family took the Oak Bay streetcar down to the Capitol Theatre on Yates Street where it was playing.

First came the *Movietone News*. In early 1943 the war was going a whole lot better. Field Marshall Montgomery had pushed Rommel back from El Alamein and had taken Tripoli in Libya. The Russians had forced the German Army to surrender at Stalingrad and the Americans had taken Guadalcanal from the Japanese. There were scenes of burning Japanese tanks and American landing boats on some remote tropical beach. We cheered. It was beginning to look as though victory might be within our grasp.

Then we watched our Prime Minister, Mackenzie King, making a speech about the war. The audience stood up and booed. Why? What was going on? I couldn't ask my parents right then because the cartoon was about to start. It was *Donald Duck*. Donald's nephews, Huey, Dewey and Louie were in trouble with Daisy Duck because they had been stealing apples from a neighbour's tree. I loved the cartoon because it was in colour and the characters seemed so friendly. I liked Huey because he had the same name as my new friend at Glenlyon.

Then the main feature started. The first scene showed the peaceful Norwegian villagers going about their business. I immediately recognized the set that I had seen at Bamberton the previous summer. In front of the church was a podium where several blonde children were dancing. I could feel the back of my neck burning with envy. David and Marjorie were in that scene. But the way the director had shot the scene I couldn't distinguish them from the other children. Hah! They weren't all that important after all. How I had resented them being bussed out to Bamberton and being paid a dollar a day, and now it seemed trivial and unimportant. My neck stopped burning and I settled down to enjoy the rest of the movie.

The villagers stop dancing when the German Army arrives on the scene. The German Kommandant is shouting orders and anyone who disobeys or tries to resist is taken away and shot or hung. Life suddenly becomes grim and terrifying for these good and simple people.

Then Paul Muni appears. He looks so dark and slimy compared with his fellow Norwegians that at first you're not sure whose side he's on. But then you know that he's the hero because he is going around the village, slipping past sentries and eavesdropping on the German officers. He's trying to find out their plans.

Soon enough he discovers that they are building a secret air base close to his village. They are going to use the air base for sending out bombers to attack the Allied convoys to Murmansk in Russia. The outcome of the whole war hinges on their evil plan. If they can stop supplies from getting to the Russians, it will make the war just that much easier for their armies in Russia. The German officers all give the Nazi salute and shout "Heil Hitler" after their meetings. Paul Muni just has to do something to foil their evil plans.

Paul Muni hatches a plan. If he can get to England perhaps he can persuade the English to launch a Commando raid and destroy the base before the Germans can put it into operation. He succeeds in getting a small band of men together to steal a fishing boat in the middle of the night. They are going to sail across the North Sea to England. If they are caught they will all be executed. They make it safely out of the harbour. But then you see one of the men reaching into his pocket for a whistle. He is a Quisling, a traitor! He lets out one short blast on the whistle and searchlights go on inside the harbour. Soon a German patrol boat will be out searching for them. Muni and his friends grab the Quisling, throw him overboard and head for the open sea. Everyone in the audience cheers as the Quisling drowns.

The Norwegians elude the German patrol boat, but crossing the North Sea is dangerous. A terrible storm almost swamps their tiny boat. Eventually they reach the safety of an English port. Once in England Muni warns the English authorities about the base the Germans are building, but they are slow to respond. They are not sure whether to believe Muni or not. They have to check his credentials carefully to make sure he's not a German secret agent in disguise. Then while he is waiting for the authorities to decide he meets and falls in love with an English lady played by Anna Lee. The movie begins to drag as Muni makes calf eyes at her, and I wonder whether or not there is ever going to be a Commando raid.

Eventually Muni is cleared and the raid is organized. The Commandos board a British destroyer and head out across the North Sea to Norway. Paul Muni goes with them because only he can find the entrance to the harbour and guide the ship through at high tide. I recognize the destroyer instantly. It is the *Prince David* with a large gun mounted on its foredeck.

The ship's officers are on the deck. The commanding officer, who is played by Cedric Hardwicke, is standing in the bow with a huge set of binoculars. I recognize one of the other officers. It is none other than Captain Godfrey, a friend of my Uncle Roy. This is an exciting movie with real Canadian officers playing themselves.

## Aunt Madge's History of Victoria

The *Prince David* enters the harbour and the Commandos go ashore in small boats. They quickly dispose of the surprised German sentries. Then, led by Paul Muni, they race to the airbase and blow up the German planes with hand grenades. The planes look as though they may be made of plywood, but I am willing to let myself believe that they are real. We cheer as they are blown to pieces one by one.

The Germans try to fire their heavy guns at the *Prince David*, but before they can get the correct range the gunners on the *Prince David* blow them up one by one. The German guns are silenced. The Commandos jump into their little boats and race back to their ship. Mission accomplished. The raid is a complete success and the sea route to Murmansk is safe for the Allied convoys.

I left the theatre feeling quite satisfied. I understood that the movie was propaganda but it was a good kind of propaganda, not the evil Nazi kind that Joseph Goebbels was spewing out on the German radio stations.

But I had a question.

"Why did everyone boo when Mackenzie King was speaking?"

My father spoke first. "He introduced conscription recently. That means that any able-bodied man in Canada can be conscripted into the armed forces. But they don't have to go overseas if they don't want to."

"Yes," my mother added. "They're allowed to stay right here on the West Coast where it's safe. They're supposed to be guarding us against the Japs. But remember the newsreel of the fighting in the Pacific. That's where the fighting is. Thousands of miles from here."

"Would you like to know why Mackenzie King organized Conscription that way?" my father continued. "It's to satisfy our Frenchie friends in Quebec who don't want to go overseas to fight. And they're right here on the West Coast of Vancouver Island in nice warm barracks. People call them 'Zombies'".

"Yes," my mother added. "Zombies. They're no better than traitors."

It was a treat to hear my parents in agreement about something. And to be so heated in their shared feelings.

*"Zombies," I thought. "Jack Armstrong ran into zombies when he was in Haiti. The walking dead. But what if the Japanese did invade some day? Wouldn't the Zombies be just like the Quislings in the movie we just saw? Maybe Vancouver Island isn't the best place for them."*

I wasn't invited to share my opinions so I just kept quiet.

After seeing the Commandos blowing up the German air base and hearing the movie audience booing Mackenzie King I was filled with patriotic ardour. But what could I do? I was way too young to be a Spitfire pilot and the war always seemed to be somewhere else. The answer came in the form of an announcement at school.

"Boys," Simmie announced, "there's an urgent need for scrap for the war effort. Ye can take out yerrr wagons and go around door-to-door collecting old pieces of metal and rubber. Newspapers. Anything. The Huns are still sinking our ships with their infernal U-boats and the Allies need everything they can get their hands on to finish the job."

I went out into the neighbourhood with my wagon as soon as the weekend rolled around. I was filled with pride as I went to all the houses in the neighbourhood. People were eager to help out in any way they could. But it didn't last long. Once people had got rid of their trash all I could collect was a few odd newspapers. Or I was simply told to go away.

My friend Jeremy Carrington had a bright idea. "Let's try the houses across from the Chinese Cemetery. I'll bet no-one's gone there yet."

I knew exactly where he meant. The Chinese cemetery was at Harlan Point right where the winter storms sent waves crashing over the rocks. Across from the cemetery were several two and three storey houses. They were old houses with most of their paint peeled off by the storms. It was the bleakest, most forbidding place in all of Victoria.

"Are you sure you want to go there, Jeremy? Those houses might be haunted. Do you think we can really get newspapers there?"

"Of course we can. I'll bet they have newspapers, and I'll bet no-one else has thought of going there. And anyway, it'll be daytime. It won't be all that scary."

"Okay. Let's go tomorrow."

The next day was Saturday. By the time we had organized our expedition and walked all the way to the Chinese Cemetery the winter light was already waning. Fog was rolling in from Juan de Fuca Strait. The tops of the houses were hidden by fog as was the Trial Island lighthouse. We knew it was there though because we could hear the foghorn. The first house we came to had no lights on at all. We stopped at the entrance to the pathway leading to the front steps.

"I don't think there's anyone at home, Jeremy."

"Of course there is. They just have the lights off to save electricity. They're being patriotic. I'll wait for you here."

"I thought we were going together."

"We can take turns. You do this house and I'll do the next house. Go on. I'll stand guard in case someone comes along."

"That's silly. It's not like we're planning to rob the place."

"Go ahead. I dare you."

That was just like Jeremy. He always liked to see me taking chances. It was just like when we went to the Crystal Gardens together. He would dare me to swim right into the middle of the pool and then make it difficult for me to get back again. But I couldn't refuse a dare. I walked up the front steps. I knocked and prayed that no-one would answer. I waited and waited. What if this house really was haunted? Who or what might come to the door then?

Eventually I heard floorboards creaking. The door opened and there was one of the most ancient women I had ever seen. She must have been 90 at least. She was thin and grey and her back was bowed. She looked at me and frowned. I wondered if she was a witch. She certainly looked like one.

"I'm collecting newspapers for the war effort."

She didn't answer. She simply turned her back to me and disappeared into the house.

I waited and waited. I turned around and saw Jeremy with his hands in his pockets standing well back from the house. He was whistling. I shot him a dirty look. Finally the lady of the house returned with an armful of yellowing newspapers.

I smiled at her. "Thank you very much."

She didn't smile back. I placed the newspapers gingerly into the wagon as she closed the door. I gasped with relief. I had braved the haunted house and hadn't been taken prisoner. And best of all I had newspapers. A lot of them.

"There," Jeremy said. "Wasn't that easy? Let's go on to the next house."

There were a lot of interesting things to do in Oak Bay when I wasn't at school or at home. There was a little park close to the Oak Bay Boathouse. In the park was an old-fashioned wooden swing and just beyond the swing there were several tidal pools. In the pools were tiny fish called bullheads. One day I took a jar with a screwtop lid from the kitchen. I filled it with seawater. Then I coaxed the bullheads into a small lagoon, scooped them up with my hand and transferred them to the jar. By the time I had caught all of the bullheads in one pool my hands were almost frozen. I stuffed the jar into my jacket pocket and walked back home. The bullheads were banned from the house so I had to keep the bottle on the porch.

When I went to examine them the next day they were all dead. I poured them out onto the grass and headed out again the next day. I went to the same pool and was happy to discover that the pool had filled with bullheads again. I went to work and filled the jar for a second time. I examined my haul. They seemed perfectly happy in their new home, but what was the point in taking them home where they would just die? I released them back into the pool.

When I got bored with catching bullheads I took my B.B. gun and a box of B.B.s to Oak Bay Beach. It was still winter and there were plenty of ducks swimming around offshore. They were perfect for target practice. I could always tell when I missed one because I could see the splash where the B.B. hit the water. If there was no splash I knew I had hit one of the ducks. The duck would sense danger, dive into the water, and come bobbing back up to the surface after a few seconds. I hadn't fired my B.B. gun at any birds since I had killed the robin at Rawdie's farm. But shooting at ducks was perfect because they had tough skins and the B.Bs bounced right off them. Or so I thought.

One day I was proven wrong. I fired at a mallard that was swimming close to Oak Bay Beach. There was a faint plop as the B.B. connected with the duck. The duck dived and I waited for it to come to the surface again. But it didn't. How could I possibly have killed a duck with a B.B.? I must have hit it square in the eye. That was the only possible way I could have killed it. Once again I had proven myself a killer. Should I go home and put away my B.B. gun forever? What were the chances of my hitting a duck square in the eye again? Probably one in a million. So I kept on shooting at ducks for a while and then I stopped, not because I was afraid of killing one, but because it was boring.

Making airplane models was becoming boring too. Catching bullheads was boring. Shooting at ducks was boring. I was getting fed up with winter. I needed a little more excitement in my life.

My father came to the rescue. He had been reading the want ads in the Colonist and one day he came home with a bicycle. It was a second-hand black Raleigh with handbrakes. I was thrilled. After that the bicycle and I were inseparable.

I rode my new bike to Dallas Road. That was an exciting destination when the winter storms brought the waves crashing right over the seawall bringing driftwood across the road and into the Ross Bay Cemetery. I had heard people say that in really heavy storms the skeletons of people who had been buried too close to the seawall were sucked right out their graves. I kept hoping to see one of these skeletons but I never did.

Further along Dallas Road was a long granite breakwater called Ogden Point Pier. This was the most exciting place of all to visit during a storm. I met my friend Jeremy there one Saturday morning and we played a game of "Dare". The game was to go right to the end of the pier, descend as many steps as possible on an outgoing wave, then clamber back up again when the next incoming wave hit. The idea was to climb fast enough to avoid getting our shoes wet.

"I dare you."

## Aunt Madge's History of Victoria

It seemed to me that it was always Jeremy who dared me, and it was always me who took the dare. Exactly the way it was when we were collecting newspapers across from the Chinese Cemetery.

"Okay, but then I dare you."

But I was the one who always took the extra step towards the incoming waves. Jeremy always had an excuse. His mother had just bought him new shoes. If he got his socks wet his mother's maid, Angela, couldn't get them dry because it was her day off. And so on.

I got soaked. The incoming wave was always too high and too fast for me. I hated getting wet out at the end of the pier. The water was really cold and it was scary. I could have easily fallen in and been swept away.

Jeremy took pity on me.

"Why don't we take our bikes over to my place. I'll get Angela to make a plate of hot spaghetti for us. That'll warm us both up."

"I thought you said it was Angela's day off."

"I'm not quite sure. Let's go and find out."

The offer was too good to refuse, so off we went. Jeremy lived with his mother and Angela in an apartment just off Blanshard Street. It was almost downtown. The reason they were living in an apartment was that Jeremy's father had died, so they didn't really need a house. But Mrs. Carrington did need a maid to keep up a good standard of living.

Angela was there and in no time at all she was boiling the spaghetti and adding tomato sauce. This was exciting. I had never tasted Italian food before and the smells that were coming out of the kitchen were delicious. I stuck my head in the kitchen door and there was Angela. She was short and dark with black hair. She was actually wearing a uniform – a plain black dress, an apron and a black and white maid's cap. She smiled at me. Then Jeremy stuck his head in.

"Angela, I want to ask you a question."

"What is it?"

Angela was at an important point in cooking the spaghetti and was obviously flustered.

"Angela, what does *fuck* mean?"

Angela turned beet red and dropped a dollop of spaghetti on the clean tiled floor.

"I can'ta tella you. Now pleasa stay out while I'ma cooking."

"But Angela…"

"You stay out of that kitchen and don't bother Angela while she's busy. Go and show John some of your comics."

## Aunt Madge's History of Victoria

The voice belonged to Mrs. Carrington who was calling from another room and obviously hadn't heard Jeremy's question.

Jeremy and I went into the dining room where we sat and waited for Angela to bring in the spaghetti.

Angela was still beat red and Jeremy was smirking. I was really embarrassed. I didn't think it was right of Jeremy to upset her like that. But what could you expect from a Protestant? Protestants enjoyed persecuting Catholics and Jeremy was bullying her because she was only a maid. But I would like to have had an answer. I didn't know what *fuck* meant, but it was obviously a very bad word and I was most curious. Perhaps it was a word for a certain kind of sin. I think the spaghetti would have tasted better if Jeremy hadn't behaved like that, but it was still delicious.

When I got home I was still wet and then I had to contend with my mother.

"Your shoes are soaked. And you're shivering. Do you want to catch pneumonia? Don't you remember when you caught pneumonia in England? You almost died. And look at those shoes. Do you realize what salt water does to shoes? Where were you anyway?"

"I took my bike out to Ogden Point."

"You went where? You could have fallen in and drowned. Could you please go somewhere a little less dangerous."

My mother never seemed really angry though. Not angry in the way she was angry when she fought with my father about religion. I think she was proud of me for being adventurous even though she was annoyed about my wet shoes.

I weighed future consequences. If I came home from Ogden Point dry it would have meant that I hadn't taken a dare. If I came home wet it meant that my mother would be angry, but not to the point of being furious. I continued taking my bike to Ogden Point and even if Jeremy wasn't there to meet me, I dared myself.

When my father found out that I had been taking my bike along Dallas Road he had other concerns.

"You be careful when you're cycling past Beacon Hill Park. Sometimes the servicemen and their lady friends take blankets down to the park. If you see them underneath a blanket you're to look straight ahead. I don't want you getting impure thoughts."

What on earth was my father talking about? Servicemen and their lady friends taking blankets to the park in the middle of the winter? It seemed highly improbable. But there was a certain tone in my father's voice that suggested that a special kind of sin was possible in the park. I wondered if the activity under the blanket had anything to do with Jeremy's question to Angela. From then I kept my eyes open as I rode past the park. I was fascinated thinking about what I might see, but I was prepared to avert my eyes if I were in danger of witnessing any sins. Winter merged into spring, but I never saw anything remotely sinful happening. I never learned what servicemen and their lady friends did under their blankets. But I was beginning to have my suspicions.

When spring came the storms abated and I found other routes to explore. I cycled up Fort Street past the antique shops and back down View Street past all the blossoming cherry trees. Cycling gave me a wonderful feeling on the warm days especially when I learned to cycle with both hands in my pockets. Sometimes if I was lucky I would see the lady with the electric car on Fort Street. There were very few cars on the road because of gasoline rationing, but the lady with the ancient electric car didn't need gasoline. She had a battery to run it. She drove her car at about 10 miles an hour and if I pedaled hard enough I could pass her. People laughed and pointed at her when she drove by, but she simply held her head high and ignored them. She was in a superior world of her own.

One day I cycled down View Street and turned left on Blanshard Street. I spotted another cyclist just in front of me. It was a lady dressed in a greenish tweed coat, a tweed skirt and a brown felt hat. She was riding a Raleigh just like mine except that it was lady's bike with the frame designed so she could get on and off her bike without being unladylike. She was riding slowly in an absolutely straight line and looking straight ahead. When I caught up with her I recognized her

## Aunt Madge's History of Victoria

immediately. It was my Aunt Madge, and she was riding her bike to the Parliament Buildings where she worked as the assistant archivist.

I rode past and waved at her, but she was so intent on maintaining a straight line she didn't even see me. I turned back up Fort Street and headed for home. I wanted to tell my mother that I had seen Aunt Madge and how amazed I was that she could ride her bicycle in such a straight line.

My mother laughed. "That was Aunt Madge all right. She rides her bike the way she does everything else. Precise like prisms and prunes. You can spot her a mile away."

My Aunt Madge was a very special aunt. She was actually my mother's step-aunt. Aunt Madge's father was Colonel Richard Wolfenden, Victoria's first Queen's Printer, who had come to Victoria on a ship that had sailed all the way from England around Cape Horn. He was a Royal Engineer and had helped to build the very first roads when Vancouver Island and British Columbia were Crown Colonies. He was my grandfather's father and Aunt Madge's father, so that made Aunt Madge my grandfather's step-sister. Things worked out that way because Colonel Wolfenden had two families. His first wife had died giving birth, and then he had to get married a second time so he could have a second family.

At least that was the way my mother explained it. I thought I understood but then somehow it slipped away from me.

## Aunt Madge's History of Victoria

"I know that's confusing," my mother said, "but you must pay attention and listen when Aunt Madge explains about our family. She knows a lot more about the early families in Victoria than anyone else does. We're going to Aunt Madge's for afternoon tea tomorrow and I expect you to sit up and listen. I know she's a little long-winded but everything she says is important."

I groaned inwardly. I didn't really want to go to tea and hear about the early families. As far as I was concerned they were just a bunch of old people who wore wing collars and crinoline dresses when they posed for family photographs. But there was a good side to going to Aunt Madge's. I would be allowed a second cup of tea and, if I were fortunate, she would serve creamy white meringues.

My mother, my sister and I showed up at Aunt Madge's home on Cranmore Road at 3 p.m. sharp the following day. My mother wore a tweed skirt that looked remarkably like my Aunt Madge's tweed skirt. My sister and I both wore our school uniforms. My hair was freshly brylcreemed and my shoes had a fresh layer of black polish. Aunt Madge pointed me in the direction of a chair with a piece of white cloth on the back called an anti-macassar. That was where gentlemen were supposed to sit. The anti-macassar was to prevent their hair cream from soiling the top of her chair.

Aunt Madge's ancient mother brought in a large silver teapot and a tray with teacups, sugar and milk. Then she went back to the kitchen and emerged in a few minutes with a tray of sandwiches. The sandwiches had a funny-tasting pink paste on them, but I had to eat at least one if I were to have any hope of having a meringue later. Aunt Madge's mother did not stay for the conversation. She scowled at us and then disappeared into another part of the house.

Aunt Madge had a story to tell us. It was about a relative of hers who had married a gentleman who was attracted to other women.

"Well," Aunt Madge proceeded. "Mabel found out that her husband was going to meet his latest lady-friend at Terry's Ice Cream Parlour on Fort Street. She waited for the lady-friend to show up and then, just as she was about to enter the front door, Mabel took out a horse-whip and proceeded to whip her right there in public. Someone called the police and Mabel had to be taken to the police station."

I was intrigued. Two women having a physical fight right outside Terry's. I sat bolt upright and took in every word. Elizabeth's eyes were wide open. My mother just rolled her eyes and looked at the ceiling. Perhaps my mother had heard this story before.

When we walked home from Cranmore Road my mother confided in me.

"You know, Aunt Madge had a gentleman friend once. But he went away to war and was killed in the trenches. It was terribly sad. Then after the First World War ended other gentlemen called on her, but her mother always disapproved of them. She didn't think it was moral that she should have a second gentlemen friend. So when admirers came to visit Aunt Madge her mother would sit with them in the parlour and make bad smells."

"What!" I thought. "*That terrible old lady with the frown and the chin whiskers sat there and farted to make them go away. What a disgusting thing to do!*"

"So Aunt Madge never did get married," my mother continued. "Her mother drove all her suitors away and now of course she's much too old to get married. She just has to stay at home and look after her mother. But she loves her work. She's really in charge of the Provincial Archives now that Willard Ireland, the Archivist, is away at war. And to tell you the truth she knows way more about Victoria's early families than Willard ever did."

I enjoyed this conversation with my mother. She was treating me almost as an adult and telling me something interesting instead of just telling me how to behave. My mother didn't have tea with Aunt Madge all that often. She was always polite to Aunt Madge and respected her knowledge but got bored with stories about people she hardly knew.

It was much more fun when we visited Uncle Robbie and Auntie Leigh in Esquimalt. We took the Esquimalt streetcar, got off at Admirals Road and walked from there to the Little House. Uncle Robbie wasn't my real uncle. He was my father's special friend. Uncle Robbie and my father had built the Little House right after World War One when they were bachelors living in Esquimalt. Then my father had met my mother and moved out leaving the Little House to Uncle Robbie. Then Uncle Robbie married Auntie Leigh and they lived in the Little House together. Uncle Robbie's real name was Bertram Robinson, but we just called him and Auntie Leigh the Robbies.

The Little House was tucked in behind some trees so that you could hardly notice it from the sidewalk. It was built with dark wooden timbers and white stucco and had funny angles that made it look like a fairy-book house. If you walked a few more steps down the sidewalk you came to a garage with Uncle Robbie's Dodge coupe sitting in it. Uncle Robbie never took it out of the garage. Perhaps he was waiting for the war to end so he could fill the tank with gas. I hoped that one day he would take the car out of the garage and let me sit in the rumbleseat, but that never happened. One day we went there and the car was gone and there was just an empty garage facing into the street.

The Little House was cold when we entered but Uncle Robbie quickly made a blazing fire in the big stone fireplace. We huddled around it, my parents and the Robbies in chairs, and Elizabeth and me in a wooden settle that sat at right angles to the fireplace. The fireplace had a huge mantelpiece covered with all the treasures the Robbies had collected. There were copper cream pitchers, wooden ducks, trolls from Scandinavia and small model sailing ships. Uncle Robbie kept his firewood in a large Indian basket. It felt really homey and it gave me a warm feeling just to sit there and look at all their curios.

When we were seated and warm Uncle Robbie went to the piano. He was almost blind and wore glasses with big lenses that looked like the bottoms of glass bottles. When he played the piano he didn't have to look at the keys. He just moved his hands around and knew exactly where they should land. He played songs my parents enjoyed like "Suwannee River" and "Camptown Races". They knew these songs well and knew exactly when to join in and sing along with the piano.

When Uncle Robbie had finished playing he provided us with more entertainment. Uncle Robbie was an artist as well as a musician. He had painted pictures of all the inlets on the BC coast and had them placed on the outer wall of the living room.

"Look, John and Elizabeth. There's Howe Sound, Jervis Inlet, Knight Inlet and Bute Inlet. Some day you will visit those beautiful places just as I have."

We all faced the paintings. At the foot of each painting was a tiny light. Uncle Robbie turned off all the lights in the living room and switched on the tiny lights. Each inlet was bathed in a soft light just as though it was early morning when the sun was reaching the treetops. Then he gradually turned up the lights so that we could see what the inlets looked like in mid-day. Then he slowly turned the lights down again so we could imagine the sun setting. When he was finished the room was in almost complete darkness.

"I can hardly see the paintings now," Uncle Robbie told us. "But it doesn't matter. I remember exactly what each one looks like. They are all firmly etched in my mind."

I longed for Uncle Robbie to do the inlet show all over again but it would have been rude to ask so I just kept quiet.

"You must be hungry after all that," Auntie Leigh said. "Let's go back to the fireplace and I'll bring some refreshments."

Auntie Leigh disappeared into her tiny kitchen and reappeared in a few minutes with hot Ovaltine and cinnamon toast. By now the embers in the fireplace were throwing off a wonderful heat. The combination of the warm fire and the toast made me feel drowsy and contented.

Auntie Leigh was an author. She wrote poetry and stories about the pioneer days in Esquimalt. When she told a story about the early days she just told the interesting parts and didn't add in a lot of boring details like Auntie Madge did. She seemed to know when enough was enough. Her poems and stories gave me a warm feeling. I could have sat there for hours munching cinnamon toast and listening to her.

When it was time to leave we thanked the Robbies for a wonderful time and walked back to the streetcar stop.

"I don't know how the Robbies stand it there in the Winter," my father said. "They have no furnace. They just have that fireplace to keep themselves warm."

*"That doesn't matter,"* I thought. *"I would love to live in the Little House with those kind people. Even without a furnace."*

I looked at my parents on the way home in the streetcar. My father was smiling and the lines in my mother's face had almost disappeared. How could the Robbies have had such a magical effect? Perhaps Auntie Leigh didn't worry about what was correct and Uncle Robbie didn't worry about his sins. They just lived their lives and enjoyed each other. If only my parents could be more like that.

CHAPTER **15**

# THE WONDERFUL LAND OF MOO

One day I found the body of a dead mallard duck washed up on Oak Bay Beach. I was admiring the glossy green feathers when I had an idea. The Provincial Museum was full of dead birds that had been stuffed and mounted in glass cases. Surely I could do the same thing.

I bought some putty from the hardware store and went to work. First I had to separate the skin from the skeleton with an Xacto knife. Then I had to scrape away all the meat and boil the skeleton. My mother reluctantly agreed to let me use one of her kitchen pots for this part of the operation. The next step was to smear alum onto the skin to preserve it. Then I filled the body cavity with putty and used a needle and thread to sew the skin together. I was careful to do my sewing to the under part of the body where it wouldn't show. I added a couple of tiny black buttons from my mother's sewing kit for the eyes and I was finished. I couldn't make the duck stand up, so I cut off the feet and sat the body on a piece of mirror. It looked just the way it would if it were swimming.

The work had been tedious but the results were satisfying. I enjoyed looking at the mallard's shiny green feathers as I listened to Jack Armstrong on the radio. One day as I was admiring my trophy I noticed a little movement around one of its eyes. To my horror a tiny white grub emerged and settled itself just below the eye. It was a maggot. I must have forgotten to remove some of the meat from the skull. I reeled back in disgust. My mallard was beautiful no longer. It was just a dead duck and I should have left it where I had found it. My mother gave me enough wax paper and string to wrap the corpse before I threw it into the garbage can.

"That's the last time you bring anything dead into the house," she said. "Leave that kind of thing to the museum where they know how to do it properly. And anyway you could bring disease into the house. You don't want us all getting sick, do you?"

I was only too happy to obey. Then I went back to my bedroom and sulked. The duck had been a revolting disaster. My model planes wouldn't fly properly. I was bored with catching bullheads. I was making mistakes in my long division homework. I was tired of the tension between my parents every Sunday morning. I was fed up with the long walks to church in the cold weather, and I worried about the possibility of dying in a state of sin. I just wished that I could be in the jungle with Jack Armstrong shooting down Japanese Zeroes.

Then one day in late March I looked out the living room window into the oak grove. A mass of white buds had appeared from nowhere. They were white fawn lilies, hundreds of them. Soon they were in full bloom. I ran outside every morning to gaze at their white nodding heads and green speckled leaves. They were quickly followed by mauve shooting stars and chocolate lilies and finally by blue camas. Almost overnight my world had become beautiful.

I didn't cut the flowers in the oak grove because I didn't want to spoil our view. But I did ride my bike to Uplands Park where the very same flowers were growing in profusion. I explored the trails between the oak trees and cut some with my pen-knife. Then I rode back home clutching the flowers in one hand to present to my mother. She was delighted. She placed them in a special small glass vase. Then she rewarded me with a glass of milk and a cookie.

I noticed that the wildflowers wilted quickly. I wanted to be able to admire them longer, so I learned how to press them. It was easy. I covered them with blotting paper and pressed them in the back of my stamp album with a dictionary on top for good measure. In a few days they were absolutely dry and I was able to paste them into a scrapbook. I even inserted sheets of wax paper to protect them from harm.

My favourite wildflower was the chocolate lily. It usually had two or three blooms hanging from one stalk. Occasionally if I were lucky I might find one with four blossoms. The petals were brown with green spots. They made me think of the colours on the skin of a garter snake. By the time I had included less interesting flowers like the buttercup and a few grasses I had a full scrapbook. It was way faster and much less risky than doing taxidermy on dead ducks.

The Robbies' garden was especially magical in Spring. When you walked out the back door there was a winding path with lilies on each side. The path led into the woods and once I was out of sight of the Little House I could imagine that I was in a huge forest. Not only that it was a safe one where I wouldn't get lost like I had in Metchosin. The path led to a clearing, a tiny meadow fringed by arbutus trees. In the centre of the clearing was a moss-covered rock. I was able to clamber to the top and then lie there with my arms and legs splayed in four directions. Even in March the sun felt warm when I lay there. The Robbies told me that this was a very special place. They called it *"The Spot"*, just as if it were the centre of the world.

One day my father decided to take advantage of the spring weather to take a photograph of Elizabeth and me. It was hard for him to get film so the conditions had to be just right. It had to be the right time of day and the right amount of sunlight. We took the streetcar to Uplands Park and found a meadow with a solitary oak tree in the middle. Elizabeth sat on the lowest possible limb and I sat much higher because I was a boy and I had to show that I wasn't afraid to climb.

*12: The Spot*

My father had an expensive German camera called a Rolleiflex. After he had taken the picture he showed me how to use the camera. He showed me how to focus, how to measure the light exposure and how to determine the depth of field. My head swam. When the photographs from Uplands Park were developed I examined the results.

# The Wonderful Land of Moo

Elizabeth looked pleased with herself, and I looked awkward and self-conscious.

When we turned around to go home I noticed something interesting at the terminus of the Uplands streetcar line. The wires made a large circle where the streetcar turned around and headed back into town. On the wires were scores of swallows. They must have returned from the south where they had spent the winter.

I couldn't resist. The next day I was back on my bike clutching my B.B. gun in one hand. The scene was exactly the same as it had been the previous day. The swallows were still there, each one with a shiny blue head and a copper-coloured throat and chest. Every so often one of them would fly away from its perch, catch an invisible insect and return. The circle between the tracks was an Eden of fresh new grass and wildflowers. I looked around me. There was no-one in sight. One swallow wouldn't be missed, and anyway they were so tiny and so high in the air I probably wouldn't be able to hit one. I fired one shot and one shot only. A swallow fell from its perch and fluttered gracefully to the ground.

*"Oh no,"* I thought. *"Now I've done it."*

I ran over to the swallow, hoping against hope that it was just stunned and not dead. No such luck. It was dead. I could tell because there was a whitish veil over its eyes.

"Never again, God, I promise you. I will never shoot another bird. They are too precious and too beautiful."

Filled with guilt I dug a tiny grave with my penknife, laid the still-warm body in the earth, covered it with fresh dirt and grass and stuck a small oak twig at the end of the grave. It looked like a real grave with a cross when I had finished.

"Well, did you have a nice time?" my mother asked when I returned. "No flowers?"

"No flowers, Mum, but I had a lovely time," I lied. "It was so beautiful today that I just wanted to ride around the Uplands on my bike and look at everything."

My mother smiled and poured me a glass of milk. It tasted bitter. I went to my room and tuned into Jack Armstrong.

When I went to Confession on Sunday morning I confessed to lying. The priest must have felt that lying was worse than deceit because I had to say more "Hail Mary's" than usual. For a few days after the swallow incident I sulked around the house feeling sorry for myself. My father must have sensed that I needed cheering up.

"How would you like to come down to Yarrows for a visit so you can see what I do for a living?"

"Wow, I'd love to," I replied. I cheered up immediately.

The Wonderful Land of Moo

13: HMCS Waskesiu, "Passed by Naval Censors", Dec. 1943

"This would be a good time for you to visit. We're just

finishing up a brand new corvette. We've got one that'll put Hitler and his infernal U-boats on the run."

This sounded like a perfect opportunity. The Battle of the Atlantic was gradually turning in the favour of the Allies with ships like corvettes and frigates sinking more and more U-boats every day. And here I had an opportunity to see the latest corvette just before it was launched.

My mother wrote the school a note excusing me from morning classes, something she had never done before. I set off in the morning to catch the Esquimalt streetcar with my father. The streetcar was filled with men who were obviously heading for the shipyards – men with hardhats, worn-looking leather jackets, and large grimy hands with dirty fingernails. There were also men who looked like my father – men with shirts, ties, jackets and trench coats. There were women too with their hair tucked into bandanas. I had heard that some of the riveting was being done by women, so that must be why these women were heading for the shipyards. I wondered what it would be like to have my mother dressed in coveralls and a bandana going to Esquimalt to do a man's job. I didn't think I would care for it. These women looked tough and they probably didn't have time to give their children cookies and milk the way my mother did.

## The Wonderful Land of Moo

The streetcar stopped almost at the foot of Signal Hill. A sign over a gate announced that we had arrived at *"Yarrow's Shipyard"*.

"Now stay close to me and do exactly as I say, and don't get in anyone's way. I've got special permission from Norman Yarrow himself to bring you here."

"Okay, Dad."

When we went inside I could see the shell of a corvette shored up in something like a miniature drydock. The noise was deafening. There were welders at work with acetylene torches. Every time there was a shower of sparks my father told me to look away. Even at a distance the bright light could hurt my eyes. The welders themselves wore special masks to protect their eyes. There were riveters at work as well. Every so often one of them caught a red-hot rivet in a pan and shot it into the side of the ship with a rivet gun. I wondered what would happen if one of them dropped a hot rivet. What if there were someone directly underneath?

It was a fascinating sight but the noise soon got on my nerves and I was only too happy to follow my father into a large room that was shut off from the shipbuilding. My father sat down behind a large sloping drafting table covered with blueprints. On one side of the table he had a set of compasses, protractors, squares and slide rules. His job was to help design corvettes and make sure that they were built according to specifications.

At the other tables there were men like him working on blueprints. They all smoked cigarettes or pipes and they all wore tweed jackets with frayed cuffs or cardigan sweaters with elbow patches. When they spoke to each other I could hear English or Scottish accents. My father introduced me. They smiled, shook my hand, and went straight back to work. Every second was important.

"The corvette has one mission and one mission only," my father explained, "and that is to destroy enemy U-boats. They use Sonar. A device that sends out sound waves. If there's a U-boat down below the sound wave will come back quickly. Then the crew knows to fire a depth charge over the side. They know if they've hit their target because an oil slick and debris will come up to the surface from the U-boat. But it's not all that easy. They could blow up a whale by mistake or the U-boat could send up an oil slick pretending to be hit and then get away. The Sonar operator has to be very good at his work because depth charges are expensive and shouldn't be wasted.

"Sailing on a corvette is hellish. They roll a lot even in calm water and the exploding depth charges send up shock waves that hurt the sailors' innards and spinal cords. A few trips out on a corvette can leave you in pretty bad shape."

I listened intently and tried to imagine what it would be like sailing on a corvette. I would be seasick and how could I man my station properly with the ship heaving and pitching like that? And what if I were torpedoed? I'd heard of men choking to death in the cold oily water, or being machine-gunned by U-boat crews while they were in the water. No thanks. If the war was still on when I grew up I wanted to be flying a Spitfire.

I liked being with my father when he was here with his workmates. He laughed and joked with them even when they were all busy. The creases and lines in his face looked a lot different from the way they did when he was at home. Here at work he seemed at peace with himself.

When my visit was over my father gave me some change to catch the streetcar home. I couldn't spend the day at Yarrows and my mother would be expecting me home for lunch.

I left reluctantly and caught the next streetcar. I was proud of what my father was doing and just hoped that one of his fine corvettes wouldn't be sunk in action. My morning at Yarrows had given me a lot to think about. I liked seeing him joking with the other men and I was pretty sure he wasn't talking about serious things like mortal and venial sins with them. "You're old enough to take your bicycle downtown now, but you have to be very careful. Remember to stick your arm out straight for a left turn and parallel to your head for a right turn. And always look both ways at an intersection."

"Okay, Dad. I'll be careful."

## The Wonderful Land of Moo

I had been nagging my parents for some time to be allowed to take my bike right into town. But they needn't have been worried. There was very little traffic except for a few delivery vans. I just had to make sure that the drivers noticed me. Actually the main danger was the streetcar tracks. If you hit them at an angle on a wet day you could take a nasty slide.

Now I could go right down to the corner of Douglas and Fort where Terry's Ice Cream Parlour was. I wondered whether I should splurge my allowance on an ice cream cone but I decided against it. They usually had one flavour only and that was vanilla. Occasionally they had strawberry as well. I would have to wait until after the war to be able to choose a more interesting flavour.

I had other reasons for not buying an ice cream cone. I had a War Savings Stamp book and whenever I had enough money left over from my allowance I could go the Post Office and buy another stamp that I dutifully pasted into my book. When I filled a book I would be able to cash it in at the end of the War, and have a wonderful choice of things I could buy. But what appealed to me the most was seeing my book slowly fill with stamps. I was a miser and I liked nothing better than filling the book one stamp at a time. If I started eating ice cream I wouldn't be able to do that.

My other reason for not going into Terry's for an ice cream cone was that it would slow me down. I would have to stand

## The Wonderful Land of Moo

there and eat it when what I really wanted to do was head down to the Victoria Colonist building; if I rode a little further down Fort Street

I came to a place where I could peer into the Colonist press rooms. They were set below street level but there were windows right at the level of my feet where I could peer into the printing presses and, if I came at the right time in the afternoon, see them in motion.

Friday afternoon was the best time because I could look in and see the Saturday funnies all ready to roll. I think they left the news part of the newspaper until the middle of the night in case there was any fresh news. The front page of the funnies was printed in blue and orange. So I was able to see my very favourite comic strip, Alley Oop, in colour before the newsboy brought it to our front door the next day.

Alley Oop was a caveman who lived in prehistoric times in a land called Moo when there were still dinosaurs on earth. He carried a club and travelled around on the back of his pet dinosaur, Dinny. He had an attractive and helpful girlfriend named Ooona, spelled with three o's. When he went exploring he travelled with his best friend Foozy, who was faithful but none too bright. When he had a problem he couldn't solve he went to a wise man called the Grand Vizier. Moo was ruled by a King and Queen called King Guz and Queen Umpa. King Guz was greedy and bossy but not very smart, and Queen Umpa was a tiresome nag. Alley Oop

## The Wonderful Land of Moo

usually managed to out-think King Guz. Moo was a pleasant place to live with palm trees and plenty of food. The only problem was dinosaurs but Alley Oop always had his faithful Dinny to protect him from pterodactyls and dangerous dinosaurs like the tyrannosaurus. Moo was almost perfect but Alley Oop had one problem. He suffered from wanderlust.

He was thinking about how he could find some new places to explore when Dr. Wonmug appeared out of nowhere. Dr. Wonmug was a 21$^{st}$ century scientist who had invented a time machine. Alley Oop quickly accepted when Dr. Wonmug offered to take him to the 21$^{st}$ century. Ooona and Foozy and the Grand Vizier tried to talk him out of such a foolish idea. King Guz threatened to throw him in jail if he ever came back, but Alley Oop was an adventurer and he was not about to be deterred. His friends thought they had lost him when he disappeared, but he was soon back full of wonderful stories.

I wanted more than anything to be like Alley Oop. I wanted to live in a warm tropical land filled with immense dinosaurs, palm trees and giant ferns. But most of all I wanted a Time Machine so I could travel wherever I wanted whenever I wanted. I loved my Geography classes at school and I could think of a lot of places I could visit that would be way more interesting than Victoria. If I could go to Moo there would be no more cold Sunday morning walks to Mass, no long division sums and no worries about my

218

immortal soul. Life would be carefree. When the Saturday Colonist arrived in the morning I read and re-read Alley Oop several times.

Then I moved to the inside pages so I could read Dick Tracy. Tracy was a tough-talking American police detective who dedicated his life to keeping the streets free of criminals. His boss was Chief Brandon and he worked with another faithful police officer named Pat. Patton. They made a great pair. Pat asked all the questions and Dick Tracy, who was way smarter than Pat, supplied all the answers. When they were out on a mission Tracy kept in touch with Chief Brandon with the aid of his wrist radio.

Dick Tracy was engaged to his sweetheart, Tess Trueheart, but every time they seemed headed for the altar, Tracy was called away on yet another dangerous mission. There was an endless supply of villains to keep him busy. 88 Keys was a maniacal killer who loved to play the piano. Pruneface was an incredibly ugly Nazi agent who tried to undermine the American War Effort. B.B. Eyes sold rubber tires on the Black Market. Flattop was a dim-witted professional assassin. They all died horrible deaths, but there seemed to be no shortage of new villains to replace them.

Dick Tracy wasn't always serious. He had two friends, B.O. Plenty, an evil-smelling hobo, and his wife, Gravel Gertie, a hag of a woman who owned a gravel pit. Somehow between the two of them they managed to produce a clean and charming miracle baby named Sparkle Plenty.

One of the best things about Dick Tracy was that it was easy to draw copies of the characters, especially Dick Tracy himself with his famous squared-off jaw. I bought an unlined copybook and started my own comic series. I was only capable of drawing profiles of my characters but, as my own square-jawed character figured most prominently and, as I could draw jaggedy balloons containing the words "Biff" and "Pow", my comics worked in a laboured kind of way. But I was no artist and I became bored with my task after a while. I came to realize that whoever wrote and illustrated the Dick Tracy comics must have had a lot more talent than I did or was ever likely to have.

On one of my bike expeditions to town I found a small magazine shop where I could buy Big Little Books. They were about four inches high, three inches wide and two inches thick, which made them a perfect size to fit into my pocket. They contained short stories about some of my favourite heroes and cost 15 cents, only five cents more than comic books and much easier to transport. Some of the other boys at school had Big Little Books as well, so we could trade with each other when we ran out of money.

My favourite Big Little Book was "Buck Rogers in the 25th Century". Buck Rogers was flying a small space ship that was defending Earth against the evil Mongol Space Armada.

## The Wonderful Land of Moo

Buck Rogers was assisted in this daunting task by his lovely girl-friend, Wilma Deering, and an eccentric but brilliant scientist named Dr. Huer. The odds against Buck Rogers were overwhelming except for the fact that Dr. Huer had invented a new ray gun called the Disintegrator.

With the Disintegrator mounted on his space ship Buck Rogers was able to weave his way through the larger ships of the Mongol Empire and blast them into oblivion. No unsightly bits and pieces cluttering up the Solar System. The Mongol ships simply disappeared after having their matter rearranged in some mysterious way that only Dr. Huer understood. The Mongol Empire made me think of Emperor Hirohito and the evil minions of Nippon. Aaaah so! If only they could be disintegrated so easily.

Big Little Books were designed with a picture at the bottom right hand corner of each page. When you flipped the pages by pressing your thumb against the corners with just the right amount of pressure and just the right speed it was like watching a short movie. After you had finished reading a Big Little Book you could trade it with another boy, and that way you could get to read Flash Gordon, Dick Tracy, Tarzan and so on. This worked fine until a boy with a dirty thumb spoiled the lower right hand corners. Then you had to start all over again and fork out another 15 cents for a fresh book.

One day I was walking along the beach and found a piece of driftwood that looked exactly like one of Dr. Huer's

Disintegrators. I shoved it into my jacket pocket, took it home and perched it on a shelf in my bedroom. In my imagination I aimed it at a sky filled with Luftwaffe bombers. One blast and they would all disappear. No ugly chunks of scrap metal and no corpses, just a neat hole in the universe where they had once taken up space. I could use it to create a perfect world free of Japs and Nazis. And then I could turn it against the Monterey School bullies. Stand aside, Jack Armstrong, and make way for the boy with the Disintegrator.

When I listened to the priest at St. Patrick's droning through the Latin part of the Mass I thought of Wilma Deering and how comforting it would be to have her come to my aid in a scuffle with the Monterey School bullies. Then I looked at the chilly blue and white statue of the Virgin Mary perched on a pedestal in a niche at the side of the church. That was who I was supposed to pray to for help, not Wilma Deering. I had better get my thoughts in order. If I died suddenly I didn't want to have the mortal sin of sacrilege on my conscience.

## CHAPTER 16

## A SUMMER OF ACTION

The wildflowers died as summer approached. One Sunday morning when my father was reading the Colonist his face burst into a smile.

"There. We've finally done it!" he announced. "The bloody Huns have taken their bloody U-boats out of the Atlantic!"

It was true. The Germans were losing more and more U-boats to destroyers, frigates, corvettes and long-range Liberator bombers. And they were sinking fewer and fewer merchant ships. Admiral Donitz had decided to take his remaining U-boats out of the Atlantic and use them where they might do Hitler more good. In the Mediterranean for example.

"We're all proud of you, Hubert," my mother said. "All those long hours at Yarrows have paid off. I think we have a reason to celebrate."

That evening my mother used up all her ration coupons on a roast. We had roast beef and gravy, roast potatoes, Yorkshire pudding and fresh runner beans followed by lemon meringue pie for dessert. I don't know where my

## A Summer of Action

mother found the lemons and she wouldn't say. It seemed like the best dinner we had eaten for years.

My father had a special treat in store for me which he announced immediately after dinner.

"How would you like to learn to row a boat?"

"Wow! When?"

The next weekend we went to Oak Bay Boathouse and rented a rowboat. It was supposed to cost my father 25 cents an hour, but the owner knew him and said he could use the boat that day for as long as he wanted.

It was a hot day and my father decided to wear his bathing trunks. First he showed me how to handle the oars while I sat in the stern and watched him. His trunks looked as though he might not have worn them for several years. They weren't stylish and they didn't fit him The fit was so poor in fact that I could see his scrotum sticking out on either side. I was embarrassed and pretended not to notice.

We rowed as far as Jimmy Chicken Island. The island wasn't all that far from the Boathouse but it felt as though we had discovered a previously unknown tropical island. It felt that way until we walked around the island and discovered to our dismay that there were crushed tins, broken glass and scorched vegetation where vandals had tried to set the whole island on fire. Practically all the young men were away at war, so it must have been teenagers.

A Summer of Action

On our way back to the Boathouse it was my turn to row. Once I got the hang of it, I found it easy. I was hooked. I returned several times and the owner of the boathouse never charged me more than 25 cents. I never bothered with a life jacket even when I was on my own. I could swim reasonably well by then and it never once occurred to me that I might need a jacket if I ever fell into that cold water. It was just like riding my bike – I never thought that I might get hit by a car. As far as I was concerned I was immune from those kinds of disasters.

*14: Glenlyon Sports Day*

225

## A Summer of Action

This was the first summer that I was able to show off for my father on Glenlyon Sports Day. I fumbled the egg and spoon race, fell over doing the sack race, got all tangled up with my partner in the three-legged race and ran out of breath in the 220 yard race. But I came first in the 100 yard dash. All the parents clapped for me as I broke the ribbon at the finish line. I may have been small but I was fast.

*15: Uncle Philip's Cabin*

When the Summer holidays began I had a pleasant surprise. We were invited to Uncle Philip's cabin on the Koksilah

## A Summer of Action

River for a family picnic. To reach his cabin we had to take the streetcar to the E&N railway station, and then take the train to Koksilah Station. This was the first time I had been on a train since we crossed Canada. The train took us high over the Malahat, past Shawnigan Lake and finally to the tiny Koksilah Station. From there it was only a short walk to Uncle Philip's cabin.

There was a big crowd there. All of my great-uncles showed up in their best suits. My Uncle Jim was there wearing a pearl-grey pin-stripe suit with a rose pinned to his lapel. He was smoking a huge cigar. My father wore a navy-blue blazer and grey flannel pants that had been pressed to a knife-edge. My mother wore her best pink and white flowered summer dress.

"You're looking beautiful, Winifred!" Aunt Clara told her.

"It's only a simple frock," she replied.

My mother looked demurely to the ground. She didn't want people to think she was showing off.

There was a pool right in the middle of the river that had been warmed by the July sun. None of the adults were swimming, and judging by the suits the gentlemen were wearing none of them intended to swim either. Only the children and the teenagers swam. Some of them were second and third cousins of mine but I didn't know them all that well. There was a raft anchored in the middle of the river.

## A Summer of Action

Soon the older boys were showing off by diving and cannon-balling off the raft and staying underwater as long as they could.

"Watch me, I'm going to swim right underneath the raft!"

We watched as the most adventurous of the older boys dove into the water and disappeared. We waited for him to come up gasping for air on the other side of the raft. We waited and waited, but to our horror he didn't come up. Uncle Philip was watching from the shore and could see what was happening. He ripped off his suit and ran into the water wearing just his underwear. He disappeared under the raft and a few seconds later he came to the surface dragging what looked like a corpse.

Uncle Philip dragged the hapless boy onto the beach and laid him on his back. He pressed on the boy's stomach and in a few seconds water came pouring out of his mouth. After a few minutes the boy had regained consciousness and, between gasps and sobs, was able to tell his story. He had swum underneath the raft and become entangled in the wires that were holding the logs in place.

"All right," Uncle Philip shouted after the crisis had passed. "There's a new rule. No-one is allowed to swim underneath the raft again. Do you all understand? No-one!"

We understood all too well. After that no-one even felt like swimming out to the raft, let alone diving into the river. I

## A Summer of Action

pretended to be tired and dried myself off. The truth was that I had been frightened almost out of my wits. I kept thinking about what it might be like trapped underneath a raft. That night I had nightmares.

We didn't take the train to Uncle Philip's cabin again. I still wanted to go swimming, but I felt much safer swimming at Oak Bay Beach. It was cold but at least the water was clear and I could see the bottom. One day I took a hammer and some nails and built my own raft. It was just big enough for Elizabeth and me, and I never pushed it out into deep water. There were no currents close to shore, so I always felt perfectly safe. Sometimes my mother came with us and brought sandwiches for a picnic. I liked it when she told me how brave I was to swim in the cold water.

My father had a couple of fishing rods he had brought out from England. One was a short stout rod which I could use to troll for salmon. The other was a long skinny rod for fly-fishing. I soon tired of trolling for salmon. I caught the odd dogfish and pieces of kelp but the salmon were completely elusive. I came to the conclusion that sitting in the stern with a line in the water while my father rowed was boring so I abandoned trolling in favour of fly-fishing.

On our next expedition we took the train to Goldstream Station and hiked to the river. I learned to cast from the bank. Once I had the hang of casting I could get the end of the line

## A Summer of Action

to make a satisfying snapping noise before it landed on the water.

"*There,*" I thought, "*is a nice tempting fly for a hungry trout. It must surely look like a real fly.*"

But it didn't. The trout were not interested, and when I tried a different location on the river I only succeeded in snagging my line on some low-lying limbs.

I decided that summer that fishing wasn't for me. I simply didn't have the patience to wait for a fish to come along and reward me for my efforts. Someone, my father perhaps, told me that patience was a virtue. It was a virtue I tried to develop in myself, but somehow I never quite succeeded. I had launched my Stuka dive bomber into the oak grove instead of waiting to take it to the park. I had spent hours stuffing a dead mallard but had neglected to clean the head properly. Running and rowing and swimming were fine, but if I had to wait for something to happen, like waiting for a fish to grab a hook, I just couldn't stand it.

I needed action even if my impatience resulted in failure.

## CHAPTER 17

## BEING A HERO ON MOUNT DOUGLAS

When we returned to school in the fall we were filled with excitement about the war. The Germans had been driven out of Sicily and Italy had been knocked out of the war. The Russians were mounting huge offensives against the Germans, and the Americans were fighting their way through the Solomon Islands and New Guinea. Every day Allied bombers were pummeling big German industrial cities like Hamburg.

By the time Christmas rolled around there was a lot of talk about a Second Front. The day would soon come when the Allies would be strong enough to cross the English Channel to France and then take the war to Germany itself. The invasion of France would be carried out by thousands of landing craft just like the ones that were used in the invasion of Sicily and like the ones the Americans were using now in the Pacific.

"Dad, I'd like to build an LST. Do you think you could find me the right wood?"

The LST (*Landing Ship, Tank*) was a big landing craft, big enough to carry tanks and Army trucks. If I could build a model of one I would be able to float it in a tidal pool and fill it with my war toys.

"I don't know. I'll see what I can do."

Days later my father returned from Yarrows with some large pieces of white pine. One piece was large enough for the hull, and two pieces were large enough for the sides. Everything else was detail. Best of all he was able to bring me an unmarked can of battleship grey paint. I could paint my LST exactly the same colour as the Yarrows corvettes. I was thrilled.

It didn't take long to build the hull or the sides but the details took much longer. I attached a landing ramp with a cupboard hinge and used thick black thread to raise and lower it. When the details were finished I painted it grey. The paint from Yarrows was so good that it took only one coat before the LST was ready to be launched.

My friends Richard Preston and Sean Montmorency were intensely interested in my project. They had Dinky Toy tanks, trucks and artillery which they could arrange on the deck of the LST. Then we launched it in a large tidal pool. It looked magnificent sailing along between the rocks.

*16: Launching the LST*

"Let's go, boys. Hit the beach. Keep your head down. Run up behind that lousy Kraut with the machine gun. Rip a grenade from your belt and let him have it. Kapow! Splat!"

Once we had secured the beach our tanks and artillery charged into the nearest French village.

Being a Hero on Mount Douglas

"There's a hole in the enemy lines. Blast right through! Direct hit on an enemy tank. It's in flames. Keep moving ahead."

"Stop shooting, Canucks! No, no! Not ze bayonets! Ve surrender!" In no time at all we had liberated a large piece of French coastline. The LST had performed its task beautifully.

The real assault on Hitler's Europe finally came on June 6, 1944. D-Day. Our family was glued to the radio. Would our troops land successfully or would the Germans push them back into the Channel? Our future hung in the balance. Fortunately, the German High Command had expected the landing to take place near Calais. That was where most of their troops were when the Canadians landed at Juno Beach in Normandy. The Germans were unprepared and the landing was a success.

"Ach, stupid dumkopfs! Zey have tricked you!" We took turns being Hitler screaming at his hapless generals.

After the D-Day landings the Allies built their own harbours on the Normandy coast. The LSTs weren't needed any more. When that part of the drama was over I retired my model to a shelf in my bedroom where I could lie and look at it. Its job was done.

The Allies kept advancing across France. The Canadian troops were instant heroes. I brought my Dent's Canadian

234

## Being a Hero on Mount Douglas

School Atlas home from school. As the Allies advanced I shaded in the parts of France they had liberated. Bulges where they were pushing ahead, pincers where they were attempting to cut off and trap German troops. A little bit of work with an eraser where the Germans had launched counter-attacks.

What a grand moment in history it was! And to think that I could have been right there in England when the troops set sail if my parents hadn't decided to evacuate us to Canada. I had missed the Battle of Britain. I had missed the Blitz, and now we were tucked away in a remote corner of Canada when all the action was across the Channel in France. I had missed out yet again. I felt a strong need to do something heroic.

"Mum," I announced one morning, "I'm taking my bike to the Brentwood Ferry and then I'm going to bike home from Mill Bay. Over the Malahat."

"Don't be late for dinner or your Dad and I will worry."

She could have been a little more impressed.

Cycling along the West Saanich road to Brentwood seemed to take forever. It was a huge relief when I finally reached the ferry. My journey was half over. What a relief to be sitting there on the ferry resting my legs enjoying the cool breeze from the water. But the toughest part of my odyssey lay ahead.

## Being a Hero on Mount Douglas

I got off the ferry at Mill Bay and began the slow painful ascent of the Malahat. My legs ached and my breath came in short gasps. I began to wonder why I had set myself such a daunting task. Reaching the summit of the Malahat was a moment of triumph. Coming down the other side of the Malahat I had to be careful to control my speed so that my bike didn't fly out of control. When I finally reached Goldstream I was ecstatic. I had conquered the Malahat. The final stretch from Goldstream to Oak Bay was completed in the waning light of the sun. My body was aching and weary. When I finally dismounted I resolved never to set myself such an arduous task again. Well, I didn't need to. I had proven myself. Or so I thought.

"You're late," my mother said. "We were beginning to worry about you. Your dinner's in the oven."

Macaroni and cheese again. Not exactly a hero's feast.

"Where were you?" my father asked.

"I was on my bike. I cycled all the way over the Malahat."

"You should have started out earlier. Your mother was worried. You weren't very considerate."

"Sorry," I mumbled.

That was all there was to be said. Surely they could have told me how proud they were of my stamina and determination. But they didn't. Well, I would show them. After my muscles

## Being a Hero on Mount Douglas

had recovered I set out on my bike again. This time I had set my sights on Mount Douglas. It was much closer but it was also a much steeper hill.

When I reached the top I was sweating and out of breath. I paused for a few minutes to take in the fine view of Victoria from the summit. Then I began my descent. It was steep and I had to make full use of my brakes. To my horror they wore out about a third of the way down the hill. What was I to do? I was going much too fast to use my runners as brakes and much too fast to hurl myself into the bushes. I just had to hang on and pray that I could negotiate the curves and not crash into the trees.

I kept picking up speed. Faster and faster. I was terrified. What if my bike flew apart under the strain? What if there was an unsuspecting car at the bottom? Finally the road straightened out and became Shelbourne Street. There wasn't a car in sight. I coasted for blocks. When my bike had slowed down sufficiently I was able to pedal and use my runners as brakes. I arrived home safely.

I was ashamed to admit that I had been so foolish as to destroy the brake pads. I thought my father would be angry with me, but he wasn't. He blamed the brake pads instead.

"These pads are made of synthetic material. After the war they'll be making better brake pads."

And that was that. He replaced the brake pads for me and warned me to be a little more sensible in the future. And I was. Becoming a hero was either too much work or too dangerous. And besides nobody seemed to be all that impressed. Perhaps I would have to wait until I was old enough to join the Air Force. But that was several years away, and it was beginning to look as though the war would be over before I had an opportunity to really prove myself.

While I had been having my bicycle adventures Elizabeth had been having adventures of her own. Auntie Bea had rented a cottage on Pender Island and had invited Elizabeth there so that Joanne would have someone to play with. Lucky Elizabeth! She was off having an adventure on a real island while I had to hang around Oak Bay with nothing to do while I waited for my father to install new brake pads.

When Elizabeth returned she was not alone. She had a kitten with her, a tiny white kitten with one green eye and one blue one. I reached out to pet it. The kitten hissed and scratched me.

"Mummy, may I keep it? Isn't he cute?" Elizabeth crossed her hands in front of her dress, pushed her head to one side, smiled, and shook her curls. This was a trick she used when she wanted to get something from our parents.

"He?" my mother asked. "Are you sure about that?"

"Hah!" I thought. "*Elizabeth won't be allowed to keep the kitten and it'll be out the door in no time. Acting cute isn't going to help her this time.*"

To my astonishment my mother gave in. " We can try it out, but it's your responsibility."

I could see that my mother was pretending to be severe and serious, but that she had really given in to Elizabeth's charms.

"Yes, Mummy. I'll take good care of it."

But poor Elizabeth. Both she and our mother had taken on a little more than they had bargained for. The kitten was cute but unmanageable. No-one could pick it up to cuddle or pet it. It would just bite or scratch. No-one could coax it into playing with wool or string either. All it wanted to do was to run up and down the curtains. Soon the curtains were in tatters and my mother had to take them down to mend them. She worked with a needle and thread all day trying to repair the worst of the damage.

"There's a war on and we can't afford to replace the curtains. We'll just have to make do with them as best we can."

My mother was always mending socks, blouses and sweaters. She even mended underwear. She called it "making do". Not throwing things away made her feel as though she was helping the war effort. Then she looked Elizabeth straight in the eye.

"We can't keep the kitten." There was no mock severity in her voice this time. This was the real thing.

Elizabeth burst into tears. My mother continued with all the perfectly valid reasons for getting rid of the kitten.

"You haven't trained it. It's wild. I don't think you can train those Gulf Island cats. They're all like that. And look at those eyes. It gives me the heebie-jeebies having a cat with two different eyes. That's not normal. You should have left it on Pender Island where it can run wild like everything else there. At least there'd be mice on Pender Island for it to chase."

My mother had a bad opinion of Pender Island. To her it was a refuge for people who couldn't maintain proper standards. She had recently had a fight with Auntie Bea, and the fact that Auntie Bea was renting an island cottage simply confirmed in my mother's mind her sister's lack of good judgement.

That was it. The kitten was either going to a new home or to some uncertain fate.

I had mixed feelings. I was pleased to see that Elizabeth wasn't getting away with having special privileges, but at the same time I would love to have had something in the house that I could pet. Perhaps the kitten would have changed as it matured. We didn't get a chance to find out whether or not this might be true. The next day the kitten had mysteriously disappeared, and Elizabeth was left moping aimlessly about the house.

My parents felt badly now and after we had both gone to bed they discussed the problem. The next morning they presented us with their solution. We were allowed to have turtles as pets. There was a pet store downtown where you could buy turtles. We all trooped down to the pet store and chose two turtles from their modest selection. They cost 50 cents each, a bowl for their new home cost 25 cents and the special turtle food cost 25 cents. The total bill came to a dollar. The turtles needed a rock to rest on but there were plenty of rocks on Oak Bay Beach and they didn't cost anything. I wasn't too thrilled. The turtles didn't look cuddly but they were better than no pet at all.

If we were going to feel close to them they had to have names. So Elizabeth and I named them. Peter and Paul. They may not have been cuddly but they surprised us with their unique personalities. Peter was lively and curious. Peter clambered onto the rock when one of us came into the room. He stuck his head right out of his shell as though he were expecting food or some kind of activity.

Paul was sullen and morose. He withdrew his head under his shell when we approached, and he spent a lot of time sleeping. We wondered if we had accidentally purchased a sick turtle. But it was too late to do anything about that now. We had made the choice and we had to live with it. If Paul mustered the energy to clamber onto his rock Peter would quickly knock him off. I half-hoped that Paul would drown in one of these forays so we could go back to the pet store and order a livelier turtle. But that didn't happen. We just had to put up with Paul and his languid habits. The only good thing about Paul was that he didn't do as big poops as Peter did. If we had had two Pauls we wouldn't have had to change the water as frequently.

Elizabeth and I shared the job of changing the water but we always had to remind each other. Changing the water was no fun at all. Every day we ran to the bowl after school to see if Paul had survived another day. He wound up living just as long as Peter.

When we went back to school in the Fall all the talk was about the war. In Current Events Uppie asked us questions to find out what we knew about the "Second Front", as the Allied invasion of Europe was called. I knew a lot because I read the newspaper and listened to the BBC News at 6 p.m. And I always had my Dent's Atlas in front of me so I could track the latest advances. It was Good versus Evil and Good was winning. We hoped the war would end quickly but despite my fantasies of Germany being overwhelmed by Allied planes and tanks it dragged on instead. The Germans fought back with great ferocity and they had a few new tricks up their sleeves. First they aimed jet-propelled V-1 *Buzz-Bombs* at London. They made a whining sound and when the whining stopped the poor Londoners knew that one was about to fall out of the sky and explode nearby. The Spitfires gamely took to the air and shot down as many as they could.

Then the Germans came up with something way more fiendish. They had a brilliant rocket scientist named Werner von Braun who designed a rocket called the V-2. The V-2 travelled faster than the speed of sound with the result that people could be blown up with no warning whatsoever. There was no defense against them. Worst of all The V-2s terrified the Londoners way more than the bombing raids or the V-1s ever did. For the first time in the course of the war I was glad not to be in England. What could have been worse than sitting there with no defense whatsoever wondering if we were going to be obliterated by one of these fiendish rockets? It would be like being back in the *Duchess of Athol* wondering whether or not a torpedo would strike the ship. The Allies had to knock out or capture their launch sites as fast as possible because there was a danger that the V-2 could turn the tide of war in favour of the Germans. And what if they could be modified to carry a secret weapon? It was almost too awful to think about. The war had become a race against time.

CHAPTER *18*

# THE PROBLEM WITH LONG PANTS

In October, 1944, I had my 13th birthday. Thirteen! I liked the sound of that. Officially a teenager and more than half way to becoming an adult. I was also in my senior year at Glenlyon. In recognition of this important milestone my mother took me to W.J. Wilson Clothiers on Government Street for my first pair of long trousers. Then as an additional surprise my parents bought me a Harris Tweed sports coat with a black, white and maroon chequered design. Not to wear to school of course. It was for casual wear.

I felt a whole lot older until I looked in the mirror. I was the same little boy that I had been the day before. Not a smidge taller and still the smallest boy in my form. Most of my classmates were 14 now, and this presented unique problems for me, especially when we had to shower after games. The other boys had larger penises and the beginnings of pubic hair. When I looked down at myself I was just as insignificant as I had always been. The older boys played rough games in the showers now. They had a game that involved lunging at one another and grabbing each other's testicles. This was called "pruning". I didn't want to play because I had very little there to "prune", and I didn't want the other boys making fun of me for being so small. I wanted my privacy.

The other rough game involved wetting the end of a towel and snapping the end on another boy's testicles or buttocks. Snap! Every so often one of the victims would double up in pain. Then all the other boys would burst into laughter. I thought that sensible boys would stop the game at this point, but no such luck. The most recent victim was in a rage and wanted to exact revenge. The other boys would laugh at him every time he missed until he finally connected and one of his former persecutors became the new victim. And so it went until Uppie came to locker room and yelled at us to dry ourselves and get out so he could lock up the school for the evening.

I hated all this rough horseplay and showered as fast as I could even if it meant I still had soap on my body. I could always have a bath when I got home. Not that a bath was any kind of a treat. I was only allowed four inches of warm water in the bathtub because that was how much King George VI and his family used and that was all I was entitled to. My mother was adamant on this point.

My long pants made me feel grownup for a while, but eventually I grew to hate them. The flannel made my legs

## The Problem With Long Pants

itch and I was forever scratching them underneath my desk. When I went to Mass I had to spend a lot of the service on my knees. It didn't take long for the knees to lose their knife-edge and then become thin and eventually wear right through. It was bad enough being the only Catholic boy at my school without going around looking as though I spent half of my life on my knees.

Showering after gym classes at school and wearing out my new pants at the knees were not my only problem. There was my schoolwork. I wasn't enjoying my classes as much as I had in previous years. Now that we were practically grownup we were expected to read grownup books. The worst of these was *Ivanhoe* by Sir Walter Scott. It was so boring that I kept losing track of the plot.

Arithmetic was even worse. We had started geometry and I had to learn theorems. You had, for example, to learn that the area of a square constructed on the hypotenuse of a right-angled triangle was equal to the sum of the squares constructed on the other two sides. It wasn't enough to simply know it. You had to be able to prove it, even though it had already been proven by a Greek mathematician named Pythagoras thousands of years before.

"What is the point of that," I asked my father, "if it's already been proven?"

"The point is," my father replied, "that if you ever want to become an engineer some day you have to learn how to

## The Problem With Long Pants

prove theorems yourself. I wouldn't have got my engineering papers if I hadn't been able to do that. Now get on with it. I'll give you a hand if you got stuck."

But that didn't really answer my question as to what the point was. Proving it was so time-consuming and hard on the brain. The only satisfaction was that once you had worked out the proof you were allowed to write "Q.E.D." at the foot of your proof. It was Latin for "Quod Erat Demonstrandum".

"Q.E.D. does not stand for *Quite Easily Done*."

My father chuckled at his little joke and I winced. I would like to have written "M.T." at the foot of each of my proofs. M.T. for Mental Torture. It was becoming more and more clear that there was no career in Engineering looming in my future.

I never seemed to be able to complete my geometry assignments in class so I had to take them home for homework. I showed my father what I was doing and explained through tears that I just didn't seem to understand. Out came his compass and protractor and he would show me how to prove a theorem quickly with a few short lines of proof. Q.E.D.!

"The beauty of geometry is that there is always a proof. An elegant solution." He beamed with satisfaction as I scratched my head in wonderment.

## The Problem With Long Pants

Latin was much easier for me. We had a master who had come to Glenlyon especially to teach Latin. His name was Captain Barry. He was Irish and wore short pants even in the dead of winter. He always came to school on his bicycle no matter how foul the weather. He was almost completely bald and wore a blue beret to keep his head warm.

We learned Latin by translating Julius Caesar's accounts of his military campaigns in Gaul. I knew that there was drama there with the Roman legions holding to their formations as hundreds of painted savages bore down on them, but Caesar wrote about his campaigns in such a matter-of-fact way he might just as well have been describing a shopping expedition. To read Latin you had to learn about tense and case and gender. In a way it was like Geometry with strict rules that had to be followed.

Even though I found Latin boring I managed to excel in it and was always at the head of the class. So much for those big boys who were forever flicking their wet towels at each other's testicles. I think the reason I did well was because I was always able to see how English words derived from Latin. Or it might have been because I was used to seeing the Latin words in the Missal I dragged with me to Mass every Sunday. Somehow or other I just absorbed it. Q.E.D.

Every so often, when Captain Barry was talking about Julius Caesar and the Gauls, he would let it be known that he had fought in a campaign himself. He never said where but we suspected that he might have fought against the English in Ireland before coming to Canada. He never told us why he was called *Captain* either. His title remained a mystery to us.

In a way he was the friendliest of the masters and treated us as though we were intelligent, thoughtful people and not just a rabble of grubby little schoolboys. He even invited us into his home. He was a bachelor and lived in a tiny cottage way out in Saanich. We were free to ride out there and visit him on the weekends if we wished.

Some of us accepted the invitation. We could see from the inside of his house that he was poor. He had a worn-looking kitchen table, three or four wooden chairs and a small wood stove. Not much else. But he always gave us biscuits and a cup of tea each. He told us interesting stories about his life in Ireland, but he never explained how he got to be a Captain. It was just possible that I did well in Latin because I liked him so much.

School was demanding, and I needed to unwind on the weekends. I had still not outgrown my pleasure in shooting my B.B. gun at ducks. One day I took my bike to Shoal Bay. At one end of the beach was a huge concrete pipe which discharged sewage into the Strait of Juan de Fuca. There must have been some good things to eat mixed in with the sewage because the ducks congregated there in large numbers in the fall. I couldn't smell anything bad so I walked out along the top of the pipe as far as I could and began shooting. There were so many ducks gathered there that I just couldn't miss.

I had only been there a few minutes when a tall man in a blue uniform walked up behind me. He had a closely cropped moustache and seemed to enjoy holding on to his jacket lapels. He cleared his throat and identified himself as a member of the Oak Bay Police Force. That was when I began shaking.

"Don't you know this is a wildlife sanctuary?" he asked. "You must surely have seen the sign on the beach."

"I guess I must have missed it, sir," I replied. In actual fact I had not seen the sign.

"Where do you live?"

"1155 Monterey Avenue."

"Just down from the police station, eh? I'm sure you know where the station is located."

"Yes sir, I do."

"Well, you just pedal home as fast as you can and report to the station. And kindly bring one of your parents with you. And that weapon please."

Half an hour later, still shaking, I arrived at the station with my father in tow. The officer was waiting for me with a notebook and a pencil poised for action.

250

### The Problem With Long Pants

"Do you realize, young man, that using firearms in Oak Bay Municipality is a criminal offense? Not only that you were using it in a wildlife sanctuary. I think those ducks are entitled to a little peace and quiet, don't you? It may interest you to know that you were reported by a lady who lives right beside the sanctuary and happens to be very fond of those ducks. Let me have a look at that gun - and the ammunition, please."

When he saw how small my B.B. gun really was and how small the BBs were his face softened a little.

"With all due respect, sir," he said to my father, "you'll have to exercise proper supervision. He can use this gun up-island somewhere as long as you're with him, but he is most certainly not entitled to use it anywhere with the boundaries of Oak Bay Municipality. Is that understood?"

"I'll see that it doesn't happen again," my father replied. "It will remain in his bedroom closet at home."

My father turned to me.

"John," he said, "you seem to be in a daydream half the time. You have to realize that you are living in a real world where there are consequences for all your actions. And you have to be responsible for your actions."

I listened to my father carefully and took it all in. He was talking about something I could understand and that made sense to me. He wasn't talking about venial sins and the

Virgin Mary this time. He was talking about consequences and responsibility and I didn't forget what he had told me.

I never used the B.B. gun again. I was getting too old for that kind of thing anyway. My father never raised the subject again. He didn't have to. Shooting at ducks was thoughtless and irresponsible. Subject closed.

## CHAPTER 19

# SHOCKING BAD TASTE

I was getting a little too old and sophisticated to be listening to Jack Armstrong after school. There were radio dramas in the evening that were more to my taste. I tried to finish my Geometry homework first so I could listen to them with my mind set at ease.

My favourite program was *The Inner Sanctum*. The program began with the sound of a creaking door followed by a sepulchral voice:

"This is Raymond, your host. Welcome to the Inner Sanctum."

Raymond then described a creepy scene set in a heavily wooded driveway, a deserted coastline or a fog-enshrouded lighthouse. A place where hidden danger and evil lurked. I encouraged my parents to listen as well. My mother seemed to enjoy it until the commercials came on.

"Singing in the bathtub, singing for joy,

Singing in the bathtub 'cause I use Lifebuoy.

Singing in the bathtub 'cause I know

Lifebuoy really stops B.O."

My mother was shocked.

"B.O.? Body Odour? That's disgusting. Absolutely disgusting!"

But it got worse. Another third of the way through the program there was a commercial for Ex-Lax. My mother was horrified. Was nothing sacred? Imagine talking that way in public about bodily functions! Did we have no defense against American vulgarity?

Apparently not.

My other favourite program was *The Shadow*.

"Who knows what evil lurks in the heart of Man? The Shadow knows." The Shadow would then discover that some innocuous-looking office worker was in fact a saboteur or a Nazi spy. There seemed to be no limit to the evil that was just waiting to be discovered.

It made me think. Was it possible that there just might be a little evil in the heart of a small, boy who went out of his way to hurt harmless ducks with a B.B. gun? That was a thought that made me feel uncomfortable.

More commercials. Dodd's Kidney Pills. Carter's Little Liver Pills. Cures for a population afflicted with poor digestion, constipation, bad breath and body odours.

## Shocking Bad Taste

"Shocking bad taste!" my father complained.

"If life's not worth living it may be your liver," I shot back.

I was beginning to enjoy being a bit of a smart aleck. I didn't have to compete with David in that department as he was still away at school in Vancouver. The radio shows I listened to on the weekend encouraged cheekiness. One of my favourites was Edgar Bergen and Charlie McCarthy. Edgar Bergen was constantly being outwitted by his sassy dummy, Charlie McCarthy. But Edgar Bergen was kind, especially to his other dummy, Mortimer Snerd, who was stupid but lovable. My parents enjoyed this program and fortunately it was sponsored by Chase and Sanborn Coffee instead of by some revolting constipation remedy.

Like Edgar Bergen, Red Skelton had to put up with cheekiness from a child. In his case it was Junior, the "mean widdow kid". And just as Edgar Bergen did with Mortimer Snerd, Red Skelton showed kindness towards a bumbling country boy named Clem Kadiddlehopper.

Bob Hope liked to make fun of other radio personalities like Jack Benny and Fred Allen. He was really good at making up one line jokes. I admired Bob Hope because he wasn't afraid to go to dangerous places to entertain the American troops. His program was sponsored by Pepsodent Tooth Paste.

"You'll wonder where the yellow went,

## Shocking Bad Taste

When you brush your teeth with Pepsodent."

I imagined Pepsodent to be like Dr. Huer's Disintegrator. One quick blast and all that scummy yellow deposit went down the sink.

"Disgusting!" my mother complained as she gritted her own teeth.

I thought my mother was making too much of this harmless little ditty, so I made up one of my own.

> "It's in your tummy turning green
>
> When you wash it down with Listerine."

Both of my parents glared at me. I was getting much too cheeky for my own good. That was the kind of thing David Beech would say, and I didn't really want to be like David Beech.

The Jack Benny Show was the best of all the radio shows. Listening to his show was like being part of a big warm, funny family. Jack Benny made fun of himself. He always claimed to be 39 years old, no matter how old he really was. He played the violin, but he played it badly. There were a lot of different characters on his program There was Rochester, his personal servant, Phil Harris, the bandleader, Mary Livingstone, the president of the Jack Benny Fan Club, Professor LeBlanc, his violin teacher, Mr. Kitzel, the hot dog vendor and Dennis Day, a tenor who sang Irish songs.

## Shocking Bad Taste

Mary Livingstone always had wild, zany things to say and screamed at Jack Benny a lot. In real life she was his wife. Rochester was black, and even though he was only a servant, he showed the kind of insight that Jack Benny lacked. Phil Harris drank too much and chased after women. Professor LeBlanc was always in despair over Jack Benny's lack of progress with the violin. Mr. Kitzel was a street vendor who had a high squeaky voice that came in useful when he was advertising his hot dogs.

"A pickle in the middle and the mustard on top

Just the way you like them and they're always hot."

The jokes were always the same. They mainly had to do with Jack Benny pretending to be younger than he really was, smarter than he was, and more talented than he really was. The other characters all saw through him and tried to kid him out of being so conceited. Every so often he would have Fred Allen as a guest on his program. Then there would be a lot of banter as they exchanged insults.

When you listened to Jack Benny you knew when the jokes were coming, and you knew exactly what the different characters were going to say. If I missed the program it would ruin Monday morning for me at school. That was when we repeated the jokes and imitated the various characters.

## Shocking Bad Taste

The Great Gildersleeve was a little different from the other comedy programs. It had a story-line which was fun to follow. Throckmorton P. Gildersleeve was the Water Commissioner in the small town of Summerfield. He had the responsibility for raising his orphaned niece and nephew, Marjorie and Leroy, with the help of his financial adviser, Judge Hooker.

Gildersleeve was a bachelor who spent his time unsuccessfully chasing a Southern belle called Leila Ransome or singing at the barbershop with Judge Hooker, the police chief, and Mr. Peavey, the druggist. Mr. Peavey had a high, squeaky voice. When Gildersleeve came out with an opinion that seemed far-fetched Mr. Peavey said, "Well, I wouldn't say that." That was a good line to use at school. Perfect for deflating another boy's argument without having to come up with a good counter-argument.

Gildersleeve was overweight, vain and pompous. But he was also kind and thoughtful in many ways, like helping his niece and nephew when they got stuck with their homework. He smoked cigars just like my great-uncles did. He spoke with a rollicking booming voice and emphasized the important words by taking a long time to enunciate them. His favourite line when he was talking to his nephew was, "You're a bri-gh-t boy, Leroy."

I could imagine living in Hollywood going from one studio to the next so I could see the radio actors in person. They felt like real families to me and I felt that I was a part of their families. Hollywood was a kind, gentle world where it didn't matter whether I was a Catholic or a Protestant. A world where my own foibles would be enjoyed and appreciated. A world where people who took themselves too seriously or became pompous would be gently reminded that they were only human.

On Saturday night I listened to the Hit Parade. My parents didn't want to listen because it was "loud, American music", instead of what they considered to be good music. Elizabeth was too young to be interested so I had the luxury of taking the radio to my bedroom, placing a cup of hot cocoa on my bed-table, and pulling my eiderdown up around my neck while I listened. No-one intruded on my cozy world.

Glenn Miller. Benny Goodman, Tommy Dorsey. I knew the names of all the top band leaders. I was just as hip as David now.

Every week I enjoyed the drama of wondering which song would climb to Number One place, which song would find its way to 9th or 10th and which old song would eventually fade away. Some of the songs were so popular that they were on the Hit Parade for a long time and I was able to memorize some of the words and, in a few cases, whole songs.

"I'm dreaming of a White Christmas..."

"Give me land, lots of land 'neath the starry skies above..."

## Shocking Bad Taste

"Gonna take a sentimental journey, gonna set my heart at ease..."

"Clang, clang, clang went the trolley..."

"You leave the Pennsylvania Station at a quarter to four..."

The war was still raging, but the songs had nothing to do with the war. They were about wide open spaces, starry skies, trains and celebrations. Perhaps they were written for the servicemen overseas so that they could look forward to coming home at the end of the war.

I had just memorized a hillbilly song called *"Doin' What Comes Naturally"* and made the mistake of singing it in the presence of my parents. The last verse went:

> "Grandpa Bill lives on the hill
>
> With someone he just married
>
> There he is at ninety-three
>
> Doin' what comes naturally."

For some reason my father seemed angry.

"I want to talk to you about that song on our way to church next Sunday."

And he did. He gave me a long lecture on the evils of "doin' what comes naturally". If people were just left alone to follow their instincts they would wind up doing terrible, immoral things. That was why a good Catholic education was important, so that I wouldn't wind up doing what came naturally. That was the problem with Protestants. They didn't go to church every Sunday, and that was why they wound up doing just what they felt like. This was why all babies had to be baptized as Catholics. If they weren't they would wind up in a place called Limbo after they died. Their souls would just float around in Limbo without ever knowing the joy of seeing God.

"There's always a choice," my father said. "People can receive a good Catholic education and spend an eternity with God, or they can be like the Protestants, pursuing earthly pleasures and throwing away a wonderful opportunity. God has given us free will so that we can make that choice."

I didn't like my father criticizing Protestants because I knew he was criticizing my mother. There were plenty of things about my mother that needed criticizing but I didn't want my father undermining my loyalty to her by pointing out her shortcomings. I just kept quiet and said nothing. My parents had problems being married to each other and there was nothing I could say or do about it. But in my imagination I *knocked their heads together* so they would wake up and learn to behave more amicably towards each other.

By the time we reached Bowker Creek my father was out of breath from delivering his lecture. As usual he stopped to pee in the creek. When we reached home he was still out of breath. My mother noticed it as well.

"Hubert, you're all out of breath. You're walking too far. You're smoking too much. Sit down and I'll make you a cup of hot Bovril. You need building up."

My mother usually took any sign of ill health as a personal affront, but perhaps she had a point. It occurred to me that there might be a connection between his heavy smoking and his getting out of breath all that time. But my mother's criticism wasn't helping to change anything, and it wasn't my place to say anything to my father about his health.

As Winter wore on and Spring approached it seemed that it would be only a matter of time before the War came to an end. We remained glued to the BBC World News at 6 p.m. The Russians had driven the Germans out of Russia and were pushing through Eastern Europe to the borders of Germany itself. The British and Americans had fought their way through Belgium and France to the Rhine River. The Canadians had driven the Germans out of Holland after a long brutal campaign. The Dutch people had been dying of starvation and forced to eat tulip bulbs just to stay alive.

The Americans forced their way into Germany and liberated the Buchenwald concentration camp. When we saw the Movietone News we looked in stunned horror at the emaciated half-dead survivors. I felt sorry for the American soldiers. They would always have nightmares about what they had seen. I had been having nightmares throughout the war myself about being chased, captured and tortured by Gestapo. And here was the ghastly proof that all those nightmares had been based on reality. The reality being the almost inconceivable cruelty of the Nazis.

My solution for the problem of dealing with the evil in the world was simple. The Allied leaders had agreed that they should settle for nothing less than "unconditional surrender". Well then, all they had to do after they had forced Germany's surrender would be to herd all the Germans into one spot and bomb them to bits. That would restore decency to the world.

President Roosevelt had the misfortune to die in April, 1945, and never got to see the end of the war. After he died the Americans elected a new president. His name was Harry Truman. At school Simmie spent a whole lesson on the subject; Roosevelt's accomplishments, the election which Thomas Dewey had been expected to win, and the new president himself.

"His name is Harry Truman. We hope he'll be a True Man. Har! Har! Har!"

I couldn't believe that Simmie could be so corny. He was talking to seniors, not infants in the First Form. We exchanged looks but didn't dare to snicker.

Shocking Bad Taste

In May the Russian army took Berlin and, on May 7, Germany surrendered to the Allies. It was V-E Day! Victory in Europe! I raced downtown on my bike and rang my bell. There were a few sailors on Douglas Street and some kissing and shouting, but there wasn't a big crowd. Most of the servicemen were still overseas.

I was excited but a little sad as well. I hadn't stayed in England to face the enemy. If I were in Reading now with my old school-friend, Freddy Price, he would have a lot to tell me about the air raids. But I would have nothing to tell him in return. The next day at school Simmie came into our classroom and talked about our victory in Europe in Current Events.

"We have a lot to be thankful for, but the war is far from over. The Japanese are a formidable enemy and they will resist to the very end. We must also feel sad for President Roosevelt. That he didn't live long enough to witness the German surrender."

Simmie was right about the Japanese. American ships in the Pacific were coming under attack from Kamikazes. The Kamikazes were pilots who were sacrificing their lives by flying their planes directly into the American ships and dying gloriously for their Divine Emperor. Aaaah So!

On the island of Okinawa the Americans were ferreting Japanese soldiers out of their caves with flame-throwers. In the end thousands of them committed hari-kari rather than surrender.

In June the Americans fire-bombed Tokyo, killing thousands and thousands in one raid. A new song made it onto the Hit Parade. It was called "Dig You Later".

> Well a hubba-hubba-hubba, let's shoot the breeze
>
> Say whatever happened to the Japanese?
>
> I got it from a guy who was in the know
>
> That it got mighty smoky over Tokyo.

"Well," I thought to myself. *"They deserved it, didn't they?"*

# CHAPTER 20

# IS THE WAR OVER ALREADY?

In the summer of 1945 my parents rented a cabin for a whole week at Yellow Point just north of Ladysmith. I had never been so far north of Victoria and as far as I was concerned this was definitely the best place where we had ever gone in the summer. The weather was warm and I spent the whole week in the water, either swimming or paddling around on a huge log Elizabeth and I had discovered right in front of our cabin.

My father wore shorts, a short-sleeved shirt, tennis shoes without socks and a pith helmet to keep off the sun. He looked as though he had either been on a safari or with the Eighth Army in North Africa. My mother wore the same summer *frock* she had worn when we had gone to Uncle Philip's cabin on the Koksilah River.

Elizabeth and I built a fort from the driftwood that had washed up onto the beach. We waded in a huge lagoon that flooded at high tide and swam in a large salt-water pool in front of Yellow Point Lodge. My mother insisted that we had

*17: Cabin at Yellow Point*

to wait a full hour before swimming after lunch but we didn't mind because there was a baby deer nearby which we were allowed to feed while we were waiting. My parents were happy. They didn't fight about religion once and, as there was no Catholic Church nearby, it was permissible for my father and me to skip Mass that week.

## Is the War Over Already?

The rocks in front of the Lodge were almost flat and they sloped gently into the water.

I could wade in slowly while the sun beat on my exposed back, but I had to keep my runners on to protect my feet from barnacles. Once into the water I noticed a kind of seaweed I had never seen before. It was stringy and kept afloat by hundreds of tiny air cells. There was just enough of it to make swimming difficult.

"Japanese seaweed," my mother explained. "The Japs planted it here before the war just so they could foul up the propellers on our boats."

Then I noticed some strange crabs with long spidery legs and sharp-edged shells hanging from the weed. Their shells had barnacles growing on them. When I went to grab one it nipped me instead of scuttling away the way I thought a crab should.

"Spider crabs," my mother explained.

"*Aha!*" I thought. "*They must have been brought here by the Japs as well. Prepare to die!*"

I grabbed a sharp stick to chase them onto the shore where I could impale them. Now that the Germans had been defeated the Japanese were very much on my mind.

"Take that, sons of Nippon. Prepare to die."

## Is the War Over Already?

Soon the shoreline was littered with bodies. The Allies were winning. When my mother saw what I had been doing she was horrified.

"For goodness sakes, John, stop it. Other people want to swim here too and you've made a filthy mess right on the shore. They're just crabs. They can't hurt you so leave them alone."

I gave my mother a sharp look. Whose side was she on anyway, ours or the Japanese? Then I snapped out of it. Of course they were only crabs, and here was I at age 13 acting like a silly little kid. Shame-faced I threw away my stick and left the crabs in peace.

At the end of the week I didn't want to go home. Yellow Point was more fun than the chicken farm in Metchosin and way safer than the Koksilah River. I was already hoping we could come back here next Summer.

I thought we were going to have to spend the rest of the Summer in Victoria, but unexpectedly my parents received an invitation to stay with friends at a place called Saltair just a few miles south of Yellow Point. Their friends owned a rowboat and, as I loved rowing, I spent the next few days either rowing or swimming. What a fine Summer I was having!

The day before we were to return home another family arrived for a visit. They had a girl with them, a girl named

Shirley. "Why don't you take Shirley out in the rowboat with you," my mother suggested. "I'm sure she'd love that."

"What!" I thought. "*Has my mother taken leave of her senses? Take a girl out in a rowboat? Hasn't the girl anything better to do with her time?*"

But out of politeness I agreed. "Come on," I said. "You can sit in the stern and I'll row."

I rowed her across the strait to Thetis Island. It was late in the day, and the sun was reflected off the calm, warm water. It occurred to me that we hadn't spoken to each other since we set out from the Saltair cottage. But what was there to say? The only girl I had ever been alone with was Elizabeth. I was at a total loss. Should I talk to her about the war? No, that wasn't a suitable topic. Should I tell her about my LST model? No, I didn't think girls would be interested in that kind of thing. Should I ask her if she wanted to trade postage stamps? No, I couldn't do that either. I didn't have my stamp collection with me.

As I was pondering my dilemma she looked directly at me and smiled. Now what was that about? Why was she smiling? Then all of a sudden I experienced a warm, yearning feeling. I had a crush on her. It was exactly the same feeling I had experienced when I had a crush on Joyce in the convent kindergarten in Reading. But what to do and what to say? Whether I had a crush or not made absolutely no difference when it came to possible subjects of conversation. In a moment of madness I decided to sing.

> "Gonna take a sentimental journey,
>
> Gonna set my heart at ease,
>
> Gonna take a sentimental journey
>
> To renew old memories."

I was hopelessly self-conscious. I had a poor singing voice, but the song seemed to fit in with the surroundings and what I was feeling. Shirley had nothing whatsoever to say. I had no idea whether she enjoyed sitting demurely in the stern of a rowboat listening to me or not. She probably had as little idea of what to say to boys as I had of what to say to girls. It was impossible. But when she got out of the rowboat back at Saltair she smiled at me.

That did it. I was in love. But what was I to do with those feelings? What if I were to find out where she lived and knock on her front door? And what if she came to the door? And what if her parents came to the front door and found a small boy standing there? Then what? I would have no more idea of what to say to her there than I had in the rowboat, and I certainly hadn't the faintest idea of what I would say to her parents. What if her father worked at Yarrows and knew my father? It was all so impossible. Perhaps I would run into her walking along Oak Bay Avenue some day. But I didn't.

My plans for walking along Oak Bay Avenue and trying to appear casual were delayed by yet another invitation. My great-uncle Osbert had died and my great-aunt Bella had consoled herself by buying a cottage on the waterfront at a small settlement at Brentwood Bay called Ardmore. She had obviously convinced herself that fixing up a cottage in Ardmore would be an ideal project for her widowhood.

She may have felt that she had an obligation to share her good fortune with relatives, or she may simply have grown restless living with great-uncle Osbert. Whatever the reason she certainly put a lot of energy into extending invitations. My family was included. I didn't really want to go. I just wanted to walk back and forth along Oak Bay Avenue moping, but I couldn't admit that to my parents so I went with them to Ardmore.

As I had anticipated, it was a week of frugal living. Aunt Bella was a Presbyterian who believed that the path to salvation was through hard work and deprivation. She was an entirely different kind of Protestant from the easy-going Anglicans I knew. She believed in early rising, porridge and hard work. She made unsalted rolled oats with enormous lumps in it followed by cold toast smeared with apple butter.

We were allowed to borrow her rowboat. I didn't want to use it. I could hardly imagine using a rowboat without Shirley sitting in the stern. Some of her guests did use the rowboat and the grilse they caught in Brentwood Bay provided a welcome relief from the morning porridge and the dreadful custard puddings Aunt Bella concocted for dessert.

Then there were chores. I had to stack wood or clear brush from the path she had carved out to the beach. The beach was perfect for a Presbyterian. It was covered with sharp stones and the adjacent rocks were covered with barnacles. Once I got into the water I was soon neck-deep in Japanese weed. But still, the water was warmer than it was at Oak Bay Beach and it was possible to swim across the bay from one rock outcrop to another. When it was time to go home I was expected to be profuse in thanking Aunt Bella. If I could bring myself to express gratitude for her generosity she might invite us back. Once we were safely home it was all right to make jokes about Presbyterians.

"But of course," my mother said, "Aunt Bella is quite right to be frugal. Think of the poor starving children in Greece."

Greece? It was true. There was a civil war raging in Greece and my mother was using their suffering as an excuse for continuing to inflict boiled turnips, boiled carrots and blancmange puddings on us. We were allowed to have margarine, but we had to mix in little packets of orange colouring to make it look edible. I secretly cursed the Greeks. And Aunt Bella.

## Is the War Over Already?

On August 6, the Americans dropped a brand new weapon on the Japanese city of Hiroshima. It was an atomic bomb.

Japan did not surrender after the Americans dropped an atomic bomb on Hiroshima. Several days later the Americans dropped a second atomic bomb. This time the target was the city of Nagasaki. Emperor Hirohito wisely urged the Japanese government to surrender. The Japanese did surrender and that was the end of the war.

August 15 was V-J Day, Victory over Japan Day. It was a beautiful summer day. I was filled with the anticipation that I was about to take part in a climactic celebration. I cycled downtown to the corner of Douglas and Yates, and rang my bell several times. This was much better than V-E. Day. It really was the end of the war. The church bells were ringing and the streets were filled with cheering, dancing people, many of them in uniform. Some of them were waving flags and kissing each other.

But somehow the celebration downtown wasn't quite the crowning moment that I had expected. It seemed that the celebration was really for the servicemen and women and shipyard workers, and that I was merely on the periphery. The war had ended before I was old enough to take an active part. I didn't linger very long. After I tired of ringing my bell I cycled back home.

Is the War Over Already?

*18: Downtown on V-J Day*

I was happy the war had ended but now what? My life had been defined by the war from Chamberlain's speech on a sunny afternoon in Reading, through our hurried exodus to Canada, my new life in the Dockyard, my father joining us in Oak Bay and now the V-J Day celebration. My elation was quickly replaced by a hollow feeling. What if there were no war to define my life? What would there be to replace the pictures of fighting planes on the Sweet Caporal cigarette packages? What would we see on the Movietone News if there were no fighting? What was I going to do with my Dent's Canadian School Atlas? I had spent so much time shading in the areas liberated by Allied troops and now there was nothing left to liberate. And what was most depressing was that I would never have an opportunity to redeem myself after running away to Canada. I would always see myself as a quitter.

What if my parents were to decide to return to England? Would we be welcome? I imagined that I would be seen as an overfed sheltered runaway who had lost his English accent. I would have felt isolated among all those people who had been bombed and half-starved while they were struggling to bring the war to a conclusion. What would my old friend, Freddy Price, think of me? Would there be any hope of rekindling that friendship or would he simply spurn me?

There was, however, no discussion about returning to England. My parents had obviously decided that Canada was the best place for them to raise a family. My father's job at Yarrows was secure for the foreseeable future and he was already talking about buying a small car as soon as the new models became available and we were able to afford one.

Is the War Over Already?

But it wasn't quite as simple as deciding that Canada was a better place for our family to live. I could tell by the way my parents talked about their respective families that my father was experiencing a loss. My father's family lived in England and I have no doubt that he would have preferred to see Elizabeth and myself finish growing up with his English family close at hand. They were all Catholics like himself, and here in Victoria he was isolated, as I was, in a sea of Anglicans. In the ongoing war between my parents my mother had won this battle. Had it not been for the war with Germany we would probably have stayed in England, and my mother would have been the one to feel isolated.

The fact that the war ended in the middle of August two weeks before the start of school meant that a fresh battle between my parents was inevitable. My father wanted me to begin high school at St. Louis College where I would be taught by priests. Excellent discipline and good Catholic values. My mother would have liked to send me to board at either Brentwood College or Shawnigan Lake, both private schools with the same values and educational standards as Glenlyon. I would emerge from either of these establishments as a well-educated gentleman ready to take my rightful place in Victoria society.

"Just think, John," my mother said, "A proper education and the right clothes and you'll be well on your way to becoming a bank president or an admiral."

## Is the War Over Already?

My mother did not win this battle. A boarding school was out of the question on my father's salary at Yarrows. And to be honest, I think my mother was really half-hearted at the prospect of my living away from home for most of the year. I did not want to go to a boarding school anyway. I had heard rumours of unpleasant hazing rituals that would be hard on a boy as small as myself.

My father did not win either. The information that I had received from my school-mates about St. Louis College was that it was more than strict. It was in fact a *reform* school for boys who were too difficult to handle in the regular school system. I stated my case that I did not want to be sent to a *reform* school. I was a good boy and there was no need for that kind of thing.

By stalling and not raising the subject unnecessarily I was able to force my parents into an obvious compromise, and they agreed somewhat unwillingly that I should go to Oak Bay High School. Neither of them was really happy with this forced compromise. They viewed *co-education* as an American plot to undermine the British system of education and impose their own brand of mediocrity.

I wasn't too happy about the idea of co-education either, but not on academic grounds. The prospect of sharing classroom space with girls was terrifying, especially girls who were going to be older and a lot more developed than I was. But it would be better than being away from home in a boarding school or at St. Louis College with a band of fanatical priests keeping iron discipline.

The problem of how I could occupy my mind in the absence of war news was soon answered. I turned to the futuristic articles in Mechanix Illustrated and Popular Mechanics. I wanted to believe that Victoria's rickety streetcars would soon be replaced by shiny helicopters landing on rooftops in the city. I wanted to believe that we would eventually be zipping around Victoria with rocket-packs strapped to our backs.

Movietone News gave me a glimpse into postwar realities. The first photographs of Hiroshima and Nagasaki showed the total devastation of the two cities.

*"How convenient,"* I thought, *"to have the war ended by a weapon that simply obliterated everything. No inconvenient junk left over. Just like Dr. Huer's disintegrator."*

But then the newsreels began showing other images of these two doomed cities – images of women and children blinded and with the skin falling away from their bodies. Was it really necessary for the Allies to have done such a thing to win the war? Why couldn't they simply have exploded an atomic bomb where the Japanese could see its power? They probably would have surrendered once they knew what they were up against.

## Is the War Over Already?

One day one my mother's friend, Mrs. Stratford, came for tea. She was in a state of shock. Her husband had been returned from the Japanese Prisoner of War camp in Hong Kong. He had returned gaunt and emaciated and Mrs. Stratford had been expending considerable efforts *building him up* with Bovril and seeing that he was tucked into a comfortable bed every night.

One afternoon he had been taking a bath. She had walked into the bathroom unannounced and was horrified to see welts on his back where he had been beaten by a Japanese guard.

"He didn't want me to see those welts," Mrs. Stratford explained to my mother. "The poor dear man was afraid of upsetting me."

*"Only right,"* I thought, *"for the Allies to have used the atomic bomb on those brutes."*

When I reflected on the decision to bomb Hiroshima it seemed like a terribly misplaced form of justice. The atomic bomb didn't hurt the Japanese soldiers who had been committing atrocities in Asia. It only hurt the women and children they had left behind at home – a gentle people who arranged flowers and poured tea. It was like fire-bombing Dresden to retaliate against Nazi war criminals. It didn't really make sense, and it made it difficult for me to decide whether or not the Allies had been right in the way they had conducted the war.

Is the War Over Already?

When Movietone News wasn't dishing up images of Hiroshima, there were other grisly topics - escaped Nazi war criminals who had done terrible things to helpless Jews, and Japanese scientists who had deliberately infected prisoners of war with loathsome diseases. It was easy enough to see the war in terms of Good versus Evil with Good triumphing. But was it all that simple? Whenever I had escaped into my fantasies of Good and Evil I had wound up substituting defenceless crabs and birds for the war criminals I so badly wanted to punish.

Perhaps there was something twisted about human beings that caused us to behave in terrible ways but only in certain circumstances. What about that prison guard who had beaten Mrs. Stratford's husband? Did he go back to Japan and resume life as a loving husband who watched his wife making tea and his children making origami cranes? What about the German U-boat commander who fired Allied prisoners through torpedo tubes? Did he go back to being a peaceful farmer in some German valley? Were there two parts of our brains that functioned independently of each other?

And what about my parents? They were two good people who had somehow managed to make each other miserable. What would each of them have had to give up to make their lives and mine more harmonious? Probably a belief that each of them had that they were right in all things all of the time.

I was thirteen and my fourteenth birthday was approaching. No matter what problems I might have adjusting to my new school, these questions about human nature continued to plague me. And, of course, I had to deal with co-education, a new curriculum and being in classes with older and larger classmates, but I had the assurance that I would be living at home, a safe haven despite the conflict between my parents. I also had the assurance that some of my friends from Glenlyon would be joining me in my new school. And above all I had the assurance that I would be able to continue my education in a peaceful world, free from the fear of German U-boats and Japanese aircraft carriers.

As to the larger questions about the perversity of human nature and the incomprehensible conflict between Catholics and Protestants, I was on my own. But perhaps Oak Bay High would have a teacher who would deal with these questions in Current Events classes. Someone like Uppie or Captain Barrie who would respect our intelligence and encourage us to think for ourselves.

I hoped so.

# *FIGURES*

1: VR1993.59.3 N309, RMS Queen Elizabeth, 1942 ................................... II
2: Elizabeth in the garden enjoying the late summer sun .......................... VI
3: First he dug a hole in the spinney ............................................ 16
4 A proud father ................................................................ 18
5: The Delaney boys taking over ................................................. 21
6: Away to Canada ............................................................... 38
7: Uncle Roy .................................................................... 56
8: The backyard, Admirals House ................................................. 57
9: Admirals House ............................................................... 74
10: VR2008.21.109 MV Weser, German Supply Ship WW II ............................ 85
11: At the Cottage ............................................................. 100
12: The Spot ................................................................... 208
13: HMCS Waskesiu, "Passed by Naval Censors", Dec. 1943 ........................ 211
14: Glenlyon Sports Day ........................................................ 225
15: Uncle Philip's Cabin ....................................................... 226
16: Launching the LST .......................................................... 233
17: Cabin at Yellow Point ...................................................... 267
18: Downtown on V-J Day ........................................................ 275

Pictures on page ii and page 85 are used by permission of Canadian Forces Base Esquimalt Naval & Military Museum. All other pictures are all copyright the author. All rights reserved

www.ingramcontent.com/pod-product-compliance
Lightning Source LLC
Chambersburg PA
CBHW070130080526
44586CB00015B/1631